Edinburgh
40 Town and Country Walks

The author and publisher have made every effort to ensure that the information in this publication is accurate, and accept no responsibility whatsoever for any loss, injury or inconvenience experienced by any person or persons whilst using this book.

published by
pocket mountains ltd
6 Church Wynd, Bo'ness EH51 0AN
www.pocketmountains.com

ISBN-10: 0-9550822-1-8
ISBN-13: 978-0-95508-2214

Text copyright © Kerry Nelson 2007

Photography copyright © Nick Williams 2007
Additional photography pages 44, 46, 54, 58, 60, 64, 72, 84, 94 © Robbie Porteous 2007

The right of Kerry Nelson to be identified as the Author of this work has been asserted by her in accordance with the Copyright, Designs and Patents Act 1988

A catalogue record for this book is available from the British Library

All route maps are based on 1945 Popular Edition Ordnance Survey material and revised from field surveys by Pocket Mountains Ltd, 2006-7. © Pocket Mountains Ltd 2007.

Printed in Poland

Introduction

Edinburgh is a wonderful city for walkers. The juxtaposition of the neoclassical New Town, with its elegant crescents and gardens, and the atmospheric wynds and closes of the Old Town, make it one of Europe's most fascinating cities to explore. In addition, Edinburgh is built around a series of hills offering some spectacular vistas across Scotland's picturesque capital.

This book contains 40 short routes in and around Edinburgh, all of which are accessible by public transport. The routes take between one and three hours to complete and many can be combined, allowing the more energetic to enjoy a longer walk. They have been devised to take advantage of views, while avoiding extreme inclines where possible, and to visit points of historical and cultural interest. Refreshments and facilities are available at the start and finish and throughout all city centre routes.

Each walk features a sketch map, with approximate distances and timescales for guidance. Around one hour has been allowed for every 4km, with extra time added for ascent and rough ground, as well as for all of the city routes – where there are many distractions! Routes are waymarked or well-trodden enough for there to be little chance of confusion.

How to use this guide

The routes in this volume have been divided into four regions, starting with a series of walks from the heart of the city. The Old and New Towns account for Edinburgh's World Heritage Site status, and it's here also that the world's biggest arts festival takes place.

This first chapter gives the perfect sightseeing tour of the galleries, theatres, churches, museums and architectural splendours that line the streets as well as its beautifully planned gardens and parks. These include the extinct volcano at the heart of a natural playground just minutes from the city centre and the Victorian glasshouses of the Royal Botanic Garden.

Looking south across Edinburgh, the brooding Pentland Hills form a dramatic backdrop to the city. The routes in the second chapter take in some of the glens and reservoirs that you'll find in this quiet landscape as well as exploring some of the hidden gems that can be found nearer to town. Linking the two is the historic Water of Leith, a wildlife corridor which flows into the city from its source in the Pentlands, via a series of former milling villages, and the Union Canal, which it meets near Slateford. Also visited in this chapter are the enigmatic chapel and glen at Roslin.

The third chapter begins with a short foray out of the city centre to the port of Leith, swinging inland to the grand estate of Dalkeith before returning to the coast to bask in some East Lothian highlights – the nature reserve at Aberlady, the broad sandy sweep of Gullane Bents and the harbour town of North Berwick.

The fourth and final chapter ventures north and west, starting just above the city zoo on Corstorphine Hill before winding down the River Almond to the park at Cammo and historic Cramond, then up the Firth of Forth to Queensferry and the iconic Forth Rail Bridge.

The chapter ends a little further out of town at Linlithgow and two West Lothian country parks.

Countryside access

In Edinburgh, you're never too far from open parkland and the fact that this can be enjoyed so freely is largely down to the many full-time and volunteer rangers who work in all weathers to inform, maintain, conserve and monitor.

From Historic Scotland, which looks after Holyrood Park at the heart of the city, to the Pentland Hills Ranger Service, which works to conserve 10,000 hectares of countryside and 100km of trails, rangers play an important role: you can find out more about their work, or even about becoming a volunteer, in the visitor centres dotted across many of these parks.

Since the recent arrival of the Land Reform (Scotland) Act, which establishes a public right of access to most land and inland water, Scotland is regarded as having the best access arrangements in Europe, if not the world. While most of the walks featured here follow established routes frequented by walkers, you should still make yourself familiar with the Scottish Outdoor Access Code, which sets out responsibilities for the public and land managers. These include respecting

the environment and private property and avoiding damage to fences and crops. As many of these walks cross working estates and farmland, it's particularly important to close gates properly, take all litter home and, of course, keep dogs under strict control.

Walking with dogs

By being a responsible owner, it's possible to enjoy some fantastic walks with your dog without spoiling the outdoors for other users or endangering livestock or wildlife. Don't take dogs into fields where there are young animals and, in open country, keep a tight leash and a wary distance during lambing. Likewise, keep dogs on a leash in areas of moor, forest and shore where there's a likelihood of disturbing ground-nesting birds (usually between April and July). Some sites in this

Scots Glossary

brae	slope
brig	bridge
burn	slow-moving stream
cleugh	ravine; steep glen
close	dead-end alley
dyke	wall
glen	valley
haar	sea fog
haugh	low-lying riverside valley
kirk	church
knowe	knoll; hillock; hillside
land	tenement building
law	rounded hill
linn	steep watercourse
muir	moor
mains	home farm of an estate
port	gateway
rig	ridge; section of a field
snab	steep, short slope
wynd	narrow lane; alley

book, such as the Aberlady Bay Nature Reserve, are strict no-go zones for dogs at certain times of the year. Keep dogs away from reservoirs and stream intakes used for water supply and on a leash near play areas and children. Finally, always clear up after your dog in any public open place, not just in the city parks.

Walking with children

Most of these routes have been designed with families in mind and, in some, it's possible to walk with a buggy. However, uneven surfaces, both in the city and off-road routes, make all-terrain buggies the most practical – and often the only – option for those walks indicated in the text as being pushchair-friendly.

A baby backpack can be a good alternative for hill and coastal routes. Most come with raincover and sun shade: in addition, make sure your baby or toddler has adequate sun protection and, in all but the hottest weather, a warm all-in-one suit, as they will be more exposed to the elements than you are.

Encouraging older children to walk can sometimes be a challenge, but most love treasure hunts and expeditions, and many of these short walks lend themselves to intrigue and adventure, with museums, visitor centres, play and picnic areas en route, as well as labyrinthine paths to explore, and flowers, toadstools and wildlife to spot.

Don't overestimate what little legs are capable of, especially when it comes to hills or rough ground, make sure walks are not too long or boggy and that you let your children set the pace. Water and snacks are essential on a longer walk: bear in mind that at some country parks, facilities are closed in winter.

Safety

One of the best things about exploring Edinburgh on foot is that it is such a superb winter destination: many of the locations in this book are at their most picturesque in frost, in evening light, even in snow, and all of these routes can be enjoyed year round. However, waterside and country routes can become muddy after heavy rain – and hill walks, especially in the Pentlands, should be avoided in inclement weather and high winds.

As the weather in Scotland is changeable, a waterproof plus a warm layer is a good idea, even in summer. It goes without saying that footwear should be sturdy for any off-road or hill route, but many of Edinburgh's streets are also laid with setts, or cobbles, which are best tackled in shoes with good grip.

For any hill walk, you should ensure that the route is within the capability of all members of your group – especially any children – and be aware that there may be crags or serious drops if you wander off-route. If varying any of the Pentland routes in this volume, ensure you are properly equipped with the relevant OS maps and a compass.

Coastal routes also carry risks. Tides in the Lothians can come in extremely quickly and care should be taken, particularly on the beach at Aberlady and the crossing to Cramond Island, where people have been stranded overnight. To check safe crossing times to Cramond Island, contact the coastguard (mcga.gov.uk) or check the board at Cramond for information on tides.

Transport

All of these walks are circular, either returning to the start point on foot or by public transport. Buses are a cost-effective way of saving tired legs and on the city routes you are never far from a service that will whisk you back into the centre in no time. If travelling with a buggy, it's worth waiting for low-floor easy access buses in the city, otherwise pushchairs must usually be folded. Lothian Buses (lothianbuses.co.uk) has city centre offices on Waverley Bridge, Hanover Street and Shandwick Place, where you can pick up bus maps of the city. Out-of-town destinations including Aberlady, Gullane, North Berwick, Linlithgow and Mid Calder are served by First Bus (firstgroup.com). MacEwan's Coach Services operates some of the routes into the Pentlands.

Trains run from Edinburgh's two stations: Waverley, at the east end of Princes Street and Haymarket at the west end (firstgroup.com/scotrail).

Some useful links

nts.org.uk
The National Trust for Scotland

historic-scotland.gov.uk
Historic Scotland

edinburgh.org
Edinburgh & Lothians Tourist Board

edfringe.com
Edinburgh Festival Fringe

eif.co.uk
Edinburgh International Festival

edinburghshogmanay.org
Edinburgh's Hogmanay

ewht.org.uk
Edinburgh World Heritage

cityofliterature.com
Edinburgh UNESCO City of Literature

scottish.parliament.uk
Scottish Parliament

nationalgalleries.org
National Galleries of Scotland

cac.org.uk
The Museum of Edinburgh

nms.ac.uk
Museum of Scotland

dynamicearth.co.uk
Our Dynamic Earth

cac.org.uk
The People's Story

Water of Leith Visitor Centre
waterofleith.org.uk

Scottish Seabird Centre
seabird.org

It is impossible to walk the streets at the heart of Edinburgh without feeling the weight of its splendid, dramatic and often bloody history at every turn.

The original city, or Old Town, is striking on two counts. First, for its position, clinging to the spine of rock that drops from the city's crowning glory – the castle. Second, for its sense of intactness, any modernisations lost in the jumble of stone tenements, closes, stairwells and wynds, and the sheer loftiness of it all.

For the walker, though, it is the glimpses of medieval life that make the Old Town fascinating. Public hangings, plague, persecution and poverty were all part of the struggle for survival in an area now lit by cosy bars, teahouses and shops. During the famous Festival Fringe, the streets are packed with visitors and street performers, but when the haar

sweeps in from the east coast, it's easy to picture yourself back in 'Auld Reekie'.

In contrast, the adjoining 18th-century New Town, the most extensive example of Georgian architecture in the world, is defined by airy streets, elegant crescents and planned symmetry.

Many of the walks in this chapter cross from Old to New Town as they explore the city's wealth of historical, literary and cultural sights. Calton Hill, home to two observatories and a host of monuments, gives a fantastic overview of the city, as does the volcanic Arthur's Seat, set in a vast royal park just minutes from the old palace and new parliament. Continue to the far side of Holyrood Park and you will find sleepy Duddingston Village while, to the west, the bustling streets of the Victorian expansion introduce another dimension to the city.

Old and New Town Edinburgh

1 **Dark Tales of the Old Town**   10
Explore the city's macabre history and visit the haunts of some of its more notorious residents

2 **A Day at the Museums**   12
Delve into Scottish history as you tour the capital's family-friendly museums old and new

3 **City of Literature**   14
Leaf through the first UNESCO City of Literature on an inspirational tour of writers' homes and hang-outs

4 **Capital Footlights**   16
Tread the boards and allow yourself to be ushered around the city's landmark theatres and concert halls

5 **The Old Kirk Trail**   18
Uncover Edinburgh's ecclesiastical history as churches and graveyards reveal the story of the city's past

6 **A View of the Galleries**   20
Picture Edinburgh in a new light and visit the homes of iconic art treasures both classical and modern

7 **Morningside and the Meadows**   22
Soak in the atmosphere of a lively student area before unwinding in the city's largest public park

8 **Calton Hill Glories and Follies**   24
Leave the Princes Street crowds behind for a monumental view of the city and its architectural highs and lows

9 **The First New Town**   26
Take in the striking facades of Georgian Edinburgh as you walk through the finest planned city in the world

10 **More Grand Designs**   28
Step back from the bustle of the city to revel in the sweeping curves of Edinburgh's extended New Town

11 **Stockbridge and the Botanics**   30
Stroll through vibrant Stockbridge, then bask in Victorian palm houses and landscaped gardens

12 **Dean Village by the Water of Leith**   32
Follow the wildlife-rich Water of Leith on its peaceful journey through the former villages at the heart of Edinburgh

13 **The Parliament and Arthur's Seat**   34
Tackle the sleeping lion from the foot of the Royal Mile for spectacular views of the city and beyond

14 **Radical Road from Duddingston**   36
Drop in to Edinburgh's oldest surviving public house before taking a radical route back across Holyrood Park

Dark Tales of the Old Town

Distance 3km **Time 1 hour**
Terrain paved and mostly level

A short walk around the Old Town, best done on a dark and foggy night.

Start at the Last Drop pub: the name refers to the public hangings that took place just outside in the Grassmarket. Head west up West Port. It was in a tenement off here that serial killers William Burke and William Hare plied their grisly trade, murdering at least 17 local residents and delivering their bodies to Edinburgh Medical College for dissection. They were caught in 1828. Hare turned King's evidence against Burke who was hanged and his body given to the university students for dissection.

Turn right into Lady Lawson Street and then Castle Terrace and along Johnston Terrace which winds round the base of the Castle Rock to the Lawnmarket (part of the Royal Mile). Turn right here,

passing Brodie's Close, named after the notorious Deacon Brodie, on the corner of Bank Street. Respected citizen by day and audacious burglar by night, Brodie's life was thought to be the inspiration for Robert Louis Stevenson's *The Strange Case of Dr Jekyll and Mr Hyde*.

Continue down the Royal Mile to the cobblestone Heart of Midlothian, marking the spot of the old Tolbooth, one of the city's several jails and execution sites. Locals used to spit on the Tolbooth door as they passed and this tradition still persists with many Edinburghers today.

Opposite are the City Chambers, underneath which lies Mary King's Close. Most of the inhabitants of this busy market street were taken by the plague which swept the city in 1645. Believed to be haunted by those who perished, the street was abandoned and eventually covered up and used as the foundations for the City Chambers, lying forgotten

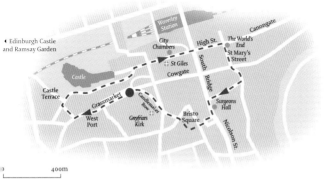

◄ Edinburgh Castle
and Ramsay Garden

until it was rediscovered in the 1990s.

Further down the Royal Mile, where it is intersected by St Mary's Street and Jeffrey Street, is the site of the Netherbow Port, one of six gates in the old city walls. These gates and walls once enclosed the city and for poorer citizens who could not afford to pay the toll to leave the squalid and overcrowded Old Town it really was their World's End, the name today of a nearby pub.

Turn right down St Mary's Street to the Cowgate. The Canongate Tolbooth at the top of Old Tolbooth Wynd was also a place of execution and would once have displayed the heads of the Old Town's convicted criminals on spikes.

Cross the Cowgate and walk up the Pleasance before turning right along Drummond Street, where you can see remnants of the Flodden Wall, built around Edinburgh after the disastrous Battle of Flodden in 1513.

Turning left into Nicolson Street brings you to Surgeons Hall, where Edinburgh's

enterprising 'bodysnatchers' delivered their victims for dissection. It is now home to a fascinating Pathology Museum.

Walk down Nicolson Square and Marshall Street, across Potterow and Bristo Square and along Bristo Place to reach Greyfriars Kirk. Said to be the final resting place for over 80,000 souls, including the owner of a certain loyal terrier (you can see the statue to Greyfriars Bobby nearby), the kirkyard contains many notable gravestones as well as the Martyrs' Monument which commemorates the Covenanters executed for treason by Sir George Mackenzie of Rosehaugh (1636-1691), also known as Bluidy Mackenzie.

Return to the start along Candlemaker Row, where tallow candles were made using the fat from cattle slaughtered in the nearby Cowgate. Back in the Grassmarket, at the foot of the West Bow, is another monument to the many Covenanters 'who went to glorify God in the Grassmarket'.

A Day at the Museums

Distance **3km** Time **1 hour**
Terrain **paved and mostly level**

A short family-friendly circuit through the Old Town, visiting the best of the city's museums including the iconic Museum of Scotland, the state-of-the-art Our Dynamic Earth and the bustling Museum of Childhood.

This walk begins in Castlehill, the top section of the Royal Mile, at the Outlook Tower and Camera Obscura. Built in the 1850s, the darkened room in the Camera Obscura captures a live moving picture of the city while the rooftop terrace in the Outlook Tower offers 360-degree views.

From the Camera Obscura, continue down the Royal Mile to Gladstone's Land, named after its one-time owner Thomas

Gledstanes. The six-storey building has been refurbished as it would have appeared in the 17th century, with a home on the first floor and a shop below.

Turn right out of the Royal Mile onto George IV Bridge and then left into Chambers Street where, on the corner, you will see the Museum of Scotland with its series of galleries illustrating Scotland's evolution from its geological beginnings to the present day.

Beside the Museum of Scotland, and connected to it on the ground floor, is the Royal Museum. This Victorian building houses 36 galleries containing artefacts and natural history specimens from around the world. Completed in 1888, the building was designed by Captain Francis Fowke and features a

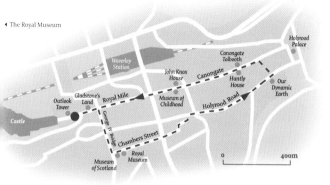

◀ The Royal Museum

spectacular galleried entrance hall with fishponds and a café.

Continue along Chambers Street from the Royal Museum, turning right onto South Bridge and immediately left down Infirmary Street to the Cowgate. Turn right and walk along Holyrood Road until you reach Our Dynamic Earth.

This distinctive building with its glass walls and gleaming white tensile fabric roof is no less striking for its position beneath Salisbury Crags. It houses a permanent exhibition designed to illustrate the processes that have shaped the Earth – and is a big hit with kids.

Retrace your steps along Holyrood Road until you reach the narrow Bull's Close, which takes you up to the Canongate, foot of the Royal Mile. Turn left up the Mile to find the Canongate Tolbooth beside Canongate Kirk. The 16th-century Tolbooth houses The People's Story, designed to show what life was like for the people of Edinburgh from the late 18th century to the present day.

Opposite the Tolbooth is Huntly House, home to the Museum of Edinburgh. Dating from the 16th century and extended in the 17th and 18th centuries, the house has been home to many different people including aristocrats, merchants and working people. The Latin inscriptions on its façade led it to be known as the 'speaking house'.

Further up the Royal Mile, in the section called the High Street, is the Museum of Childhood, the first ever museum, when it opened in 1955, to specialise in the history of childhood: it is packed with toys and games from around the world.

Directly opposite is John Knox House Museum where the leader of the Scottish Reformation and founder of the Presbyterian Church lived for a short while before his death in 1572. From here, you can continue back up to Castlehill.

City of Literature

Distance **3km** Time **1 hour**
Terrain **paved and mostly level, steps, a climb to gain the castle**

A great route for bookworms as it travels from Old Town to New Town in search of literary references and inspiration.

From the foot of The Mound, turn left into West Princes Street Gardens and go down the steps beside the floral clock. Veer left to curve down past a lodge and, when you reach the bottom, carry straight on through the centre of the gardens.

Turn left before the Ross Bandstand to skirt behind it and cross a footbridge over the railway. Take the second left up a flight of steps, bearing right at a fork to enjoy fine views of Princes Street as you zigzag uphill under Castle Rock. At the next fork, follow the higher path (right) towards Ramsay Garden and the Castle Esplanade.

Leave the Esplanade down the Royal Mile, turning left into Ramsay Lane and then left again into Ramsay Garden.

Ramsay Garden was built around Ramsay Lodge, the octagonal retirement home of the poet Allan Ramsay (1686-1758). A bookseller and publisher as well as a poet, Ramsay opened what is thought to be the first lending library in Britain in the High Street near St Giles in 1725.

Continue down Ramsay Lane as it winds past Patrick Geddes Hall and the Assembly Hall, built in 1859 for the breakaway Free Church of Scotland. Turn sharp right to climb a flight of stone steps into the atmospheric Mylne's Court, one of old Edinburgh's first open squares.

Emerge briefly onto the Royal Mile only to dive left down James Court West Entry. Once the fashionable hub of the city, David Hume, James Boswell, Samuel Johnson and Robert Burns all stayed here at one time or another.

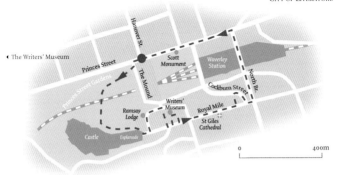

◀ The Writers' Museum

A right turn takes you across James Court, skirting behind Gladstone's Land to arrive at the Writers' Museum in Lady Stair's Close, which commemorates the work of Sir Walter Scott and Robert Louis Stevenson as well as Burns. The museum is housed in the mansion of Lady Stair, built in 1622.

Just beyond is Wardrop's Court, part of which has been designated Makars' Court, which derives its name from the Scots word for 'poet'. Around the court are inscribed flagstones celebrating the works of Scottish writers from the 14th century to the present day, as an 'evolving national literary monument'.

Leave the court by Wardrop's Close and turn left down the Royal Mile. In St Giles Cathedral, there is a low-relief memorial to Stevenson, cast in bronze in 1904 by American sculptor Augustus St Gaudens. The great west window or Burns window was installed in 1985 and is the work of the Icelandic artist Leifur Breidfjörd.

Continue down the Royal Mile before ducking down Anchor Close (left), once home to Smellie's Printing House. William Smellie (1740-1795) was a printer, antiquarian and naturalist who printed the first edition of the *Encyclopaedia Britannica* in 1771. The close was also home to Dawney Douglas's tavern, the meeting place of the Crochallan Fencibles, a drinking club started by Smellie in 1718 and frequented by Burns.

Turn right up Cockburn Street and left into the Royal Mile again. It's a left turn to cross North Bridge and then left again along Princes Street, where you will see the Gothic Scott Monument towering in front of you. Designed by George Meikle Kemp (1795-1844) and opened in 1846, this 61m-high structure offers commanding views of the city from the top.

Further along Princes Street, you can detour up Hanover Street (right) to the corner of Rose Street, where you will see Milne's Bar, the former haunt of several of Scotland's most influential modern poets including Hugh MacDiarmid (1892-1978), Norman MacCaig (1910-1996) and Sorley MacLean (1911-1996). Return to The Mound.

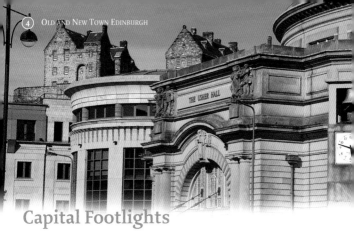

Capital Footlights

Distance 6.5km Time 2 hours
Terrain paved and level, steps at end

A tour of Edinburgh's theatres, starting with the copper-domed Usher Hall and its neighbour the Royal Lyceum Theatre.

Lothian Road is home to several cultural venues, including the Usher Hall, Royal Lyceum Theatre, Traverse Theatre and Filmhouse Cinema, all within shouting distance of one another. It's a short stroll south from the west end of Princes Street and a 15-minute walk from Haymarket Station to the landmark Usher Hall.

Built in 1914, as a gift to the city from brewer and distiller Andrew Usher, this is Edinburgh's main concert venue. The round building has a copper-domed roof and is decorated with sculptures. Next to it is the Royal Lyceum Theatre (1883). Built for J B Howard and F W P Wyndham, renowned figures in the Edinburgh theatrical world, it has managed to remain largely unaltered over the years.

Further up Lothian Road, The King's Theatre, also built for Howard and Wyndham, with an exquisite interior, focused more on variety performances when it opened in 1906.

From behind the King's, cross the Meadows to Edinburgh's Southside. In Clerk Street, the main thoroughfare, you will find the Queens Hall. Originally a Georgian church, it was transformed into a concert hall in the late 1970s and is now home to the Scottish Chamber Orchestra.

Walking north brings you to the Festival Theatre, which opened in 1994 on the site of the lavish Empire Palace Theatre (1892). This venue, which mixes elements of art nouveau, beaux arts and neo-classicism, with a modern glass frontage, is said to be haunted by the ghost of the illusionist The Great Lafayette, who died at the Empire in a tragic stage fire in 1911.

Continue north onto South Bridge, then right along Infirmary Street and left down Robertson's Close to the Cowgate, where

◀ The Usher Hall

you will find St Cecilia's Hall (1763). Designed by Robert Mylne for the Musical Society of Edinburgh, it is the oldest purpose-built concert hall in Scotland. Partially hidden by South Bridge, this once fashionable venue was bought by Edinburgh University in the 1960s and restored to house a collection of harpsichords and clavichords.

Walk up Niddry Street and turn right down the Royal Mile (High Street) to the Scottish Storytelling Centre, which has a court for performance and gathering. Further down, turn left into New Street, left again onto Calton Road and right down Leith Street. Edinburgh Playhouse, at the top of Leith Walk, was designed as a variety theatre, but for its first 40 years was used as a cinema. Today it stages musicals, dance, opera and concerts.

Return up Leith Street and west along Princes Street to the Ross Open Air Theatre in West Princes Street Gardens. The Ross Bandstand, as it is better known,

hosts the musical accompaniment to the annual fireworks display during the Edinburgh International Festival.

Continue past the ornate 19th-century Ross Fountain and over the footbridge to exit onto King's Stables Road where a steep flight of steps takes you to the modern Traverse Theatre, which stages contemporary drama and dance. Just in front of this is Usher Hall.

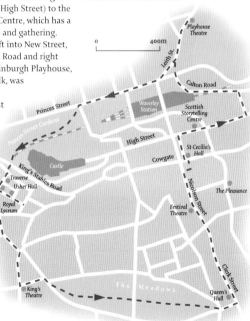

The Old Kirk Trail

Distance **6.5km** Time **2 hours**
Terrain **paved and mostly level**

**A long walk from medieval to Georgian
Edinburgh, visiting some of the city's
most prominent and interesting kirks
and cemeteries.**

This walk starts at St Giles in the heart
of the Old Town. Founded in the 1120s as a
Catholic church, St Giles became a
Protestant place of worship after the
Reformation and John Knox, leader of the
Scottish Reformation, served as minister
until 1570. The Reformers split the interior
and used it for a range of purposes
including police station, fire station,
school and prison for prostitutes.

Further down the High Street, on the
right, is the landmark Tron Kirk. Now a
visitor centre, it was used for worship
from 1648 to 1952. In 1974, an
archaeological excavation under the
church floor exposed a 'lost' 16th-century
street called Marlin's Wynd, Edinburgh's
oldest surviving paved street.

Pass the John Knox House as you
continue downhill to the Canongate Kirk
(1691), built for the Presbyterian
congregation when the Abbey Church of
Holyrood was converted into a chapel.

At the foot of the Royal Mile, beside the
medieval ruins of Holyrood Abbey, lies the
magnificent Holyrood Palace, the Queen's
official residence in Scotland. Dating from
the early 16th century, its construction was
initiated by James IV and it was later home
to Mary Queen of Scots. From the palace
gates, turn left up
Holyrood Road and on
through the Cowgate

to Magdalen Chapel. Small and easily missed, this building was completed in 1544 and is home to some beautiful examples of pre-reformation stained glass.

Shortly after, turn left up Candlemaker Row to Greyfriars Tolbooth and Highland Kirk (1620), otherwise known as Greyfriars, the first church built in Edinburgh after the Reformation. Standing on ground that was outside the 16th-century city, parts of the Flodden Wall and Telfer Wall can be seen in the kirkyard. The National Covenant was signed in front of the pulpit in 1638, and in 1679 around 1200 Covenanters were imprisoned in terrible conditions in the kirkyard.

Return down Candlemaker Row, through the Grassmarket and along King's Stables Road to St Cuthbert's Church. You'll see a circular watchtower, which dates from the days when the occupants had to be guarded from Edinburgh's graverobbers. Beside St Cuthbert's is the towering St John's, designed by William Burn (1789-1870) and worth visiting for its ornate interior, a welcome respite from the bustle of the main thoroughfare outside.

Cross Princes Street to walk down Queensferry Street then turn left into Melville Street, at the end of which is the splendid St Mary's Episcopalian Cathedral, designed by Sir George Gilbert Scott.

Return to Queensferry Street via the fashionable Drumsheugh Gardens and cross the Dean Bridge, before turning right into Dean Park Crescent and right again into the elegant Ann Street, named after the wife of painter Henry Raeburn, who designed it. Unlike other streets in the New Town, these houses have front gardens. Ann Street curves round into Dean Terrace, a pretty cobbled street overlooking the Water of Leith.

Turn right into Deanhaugh Street and left into St Stephen's Street to find the churches of St Stephen, designed on an awkward slope by W H Playfair, and St Vincent. Walk up Howe Street to George Street where you will find St Andrew's and St George's Church (1784), the New Town's first place of worship. From here, you can walk up Hanover Street and cross Princes Street to return up The Mound to St Giles.

◀ St Giles Cathedral

A View of the Galleries

Distance **5.5km** Time **2 hours**
Terrain **mostly paved and level, avoidable steps at start and on Water of Leith Walkway, which can also be muddy**

A stroll around Edinburgh's public and private art galleries, passing from Old to New Town, through Stockbridge and along the Water of Leith. The free National Galleries bus completes the circuit.

Market Street, at the back of Waverley Station, is home to two of the city's art galleries, the City Art Centre and the Fruitmarket Gallery. Built as a fruit and vegetable market in 1938, the latter building became an art gallery after the Scottish Arts Council saved it from demolition in 1974. Opened in 1980, the City Art Centre houses some of the city's collection of Scottish art as well as playing host to an eclectic mixture of exhibitions. Both are easily reached from Princes Street via Waverley Bridge or from the railway station's upper walkway on the south side.

From the top of Market Street, turn right down the Playfair Steps where you will find the National Gallery of Scotland, home to European paintings and sculpture from the Renaissance to Post-Impressionism. The building was designed by W H Playfair (1790-1857) and was opened to the public in 1859. Directly in front of the National Gallery is the Royal Scottish Academy (RSA), also designed by Playfair and opened in 1826. The RSA is home to the Diploma Collection of drawings and models, works by recipients of RSA scholarships and copies of Old Masters.

Leave the RSA by the front entrance on Princes Street and turn right into East

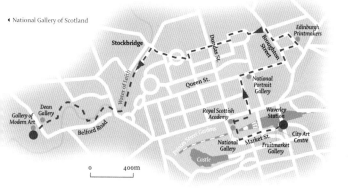

◀ National Gallery of Scotland

Stockbridge

Dundas St.

Broughton Street

Edinburgh Printmakers

Queen St.

National Portrait Gallery

Water of Leith

Dean Gallery

Gallery of Modern Art

Belford Road

Royal Scottish Academy

Waverley Station

City Art Centre

National Gallery

Market St.

Fruitmarket Gallery

Castle

Princes Street Gardens

0   400m

Princes Street Gardens, where you will get a good view of the two galleries and the more recent subterranean Weston Link, with its lecture theatre, restaurant, café and shop. Walk eastwards through the gardens to the Scott Monument, then cross Princes Street and walk the length of St David Street, before turning right into Queen Street where you will find the Scottish National Portrait Gallery. This contains portraits of Scots who have shaped the development of the country and includes works by Van Dyck, Gainsborough and Rodin as well as Scottish artists such as Ramsay and Raeburn. Continue east along Queen Street into York Place, once home to Alexander Nasmyth and Sir Henry Raeburn, before turning left into Broughton Street, right into Forth Street and then left down Union Street. Here, you will find the Edinburgh Printmakers

Workshop and Gallery on the right. The first open-access print studio in Britain, the workshop provides etching, lithography, screen-printing and relief printing facilities for artists. Entry is free and there is a viewing window where you can watch the artists at work.

From here, turn left along Broughton Place to Broughton Street. At the foot of this street, take a left off the roundabout to London Street, Drummond Place and Great King Street. Cross Dundas Street, home to many private galleries and antique shops, and carry on along Great King Street into Circus Place and down to Hamilton Place. Turn left along Saunders Street to access the peaceful Water of Leith Walkway. This leads through the picturesque Dean Village to the Dean Gallery and Gallery of Modern Art just beyond. Return to The Mound by the free National Galleries bus.

Morningside and the Meadows

Distance 4km **Time** 1 hour 30 **Terrain** paved and mostly level **Access** bus (11, 15, 16, 23) to Morningside

A browse through Morningside's quirky shops, lingering in Bruntsfield Links and the Meadows before reaching the Old Town's photogenic West Bow.

Start at the clock at the foot of Morningside Road some 2km south of the west end of Princes Street (regular buses). This marks the site of Morningside Station, whose arrival in 1884 helped transform a secluded village into a desirable city suburb.

Walk north up the main thoroughfare, passing Jordan Lane and Canaan Lane in the area sometimes known as Little Egypt. On Nile Grove sits the octagonal Braid Church, designed by George Washington Browne and opened in 1887.

Further up Morningside Road on the right, you pass The Canny Man's public house. Until the 1850s, it was a stopping-off point for farmers and drovers on their way to Edinburgh. Bought by James Kerr in 1871, it was named The Volunteer Arms, as it was popular with the Edinburgh Volunteers, later to become the Edinburgh and Midlothian Rifle Association. The current name comes from the steadying influence Kerr had on the carters who frequented it. Beyond this, on the left, you will see Spring Valley Gardens, once home to Reid's Byres, a dairy farm demolished in 1899 and Morningside Public Hall, later a cinema and ballroom.

A little further on are Morningside Library, opened in 1904 and extended in 1929, and The Old Schoolhouse, opened in 1823 but closed in 1892 when South Morningside Primary opened. On the opposite side of the road, on the corner of Newbattle Terrace, stands a small church, now part of Napier University. At the top of the hill on the right is Church Hill Theatre,

◀ Victoria Street

formerly Morningside High Church.

Morningside Road ends at the junction with Colinton Road and Chamberlain Road, or Holy Corner as it is known, because of the churches that stand on each of these four corners.

Continue along the main road, now Bruntsfield Place, with its assortment of shops, into Bruntsfield, a lively residential district favoured by students and young professionals. Look down Viewforth and Leamington Terrace on the left for good views of the city and Fife. At Bruntsfield Links, take the footpath/cycleway on the right to cut across the edge of the links, crossing Whitehouse Loan and continuing (right) to skirt the links. Across the grass to your left is the Golf Tavern and beside it the Barclay Church, built by Frederick Thomas Pilkington in 1862-4, with its huge spire dominating the skyline. Beyond you can see the castle while in front of you are Salisbury Crags.

As you continue through Bruntsfield Links, you can see Marchmont on the right, another popular student area as it falls between the campuses of Edinburgh and Napier Universities.

Where the path meets Marchmont Road, turn right, then left along Warrender Park Road. Carry straight on until you reach Argyle Place, then turn left along this. At the bottom, cross Melville Drive to continue north through the Meadows on Middle Meadow Walk. Salisbury Crags and Arthur's Seat are now to your right while ahead is the old Royal Infirmary. At the top of Middle Meadow Walk, cross the road and go straight down Forrest Road to reach George IV Bridge (buses back to Morningside) and Victoria Street, an interesting galleried shopping street that curves down to the Grassmarket.

Calton Hill Glories and Follies

Distance **4km** Time **1 hour 30**
Terrain **moderately hilly, steps to start**

Edinburgh's classic city hilltop circuit, which offers one of the best perspectives of the Old Town skyline and returns by the Georgian streets that lie beneath.

A trip up Calton Hill can be particularly rewarding at sunset, when the views of the castle, the spires of the Old Town and Princes Street are stunning. The hill is also home to the exuberant pagan fire festival of Beltane which takes place on the last night of April every year.

Start at the entrance to Calton Hill on Regent Road, a short distance from Waverley Station and Princes Street. (From Waverley Steps, turn right to pass the Balmoral Hotel and cross North

Bridge, branching right along Waterloo Place. The entrance is on the left.)

Climb the steps and wide path straight ahead. On your left are views across the north of the city to the Firth of Forth and beyond to Fife. The path now contours round to the right with an outlook over the port of Leith and, as it curves round behind the National Monument, gives views over the palace and parliament to Holyrood Park beyond.

The National Monument was designed by Charles Robert Cockerell and William Henry Playfair in the image of the Parthenon in honour of those who died in the Napoleonic Wars. Known as Edinburgh's Disgrace, there is some dispute as to whether it was unfinished due to lack of funds or was intended to

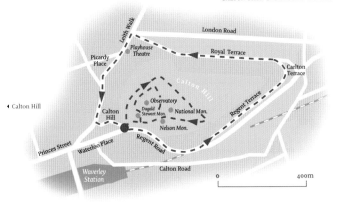

◀ Calton Hill

look as it does. The path now brings you between the National Monument and the Nelson Monument.

The Nelson Monument commemorates the victory and death of Lord Admiral Nelson at the battle of Trafalgar in 1805. Completed in 1815, the monument was designed by Robert Burn in the shape of an upturned telescope. The time ball was introduced in 1852 and, during summer hours, it is lowered to coincide with the firing of the one o'clock gun at the castle.

For a short, fairly level hilltop circuit with panoramic views, follow the path around the side of the City Observatory and above the circular, colonnaded Dugald Stewart Monument, designed by Playfair. Here you will find the Old Observatory, designed by New Town architect James Craig in 1792.

After returning to the front of the Observatory, you can take the path below the Dugald Stewart Monument down the steep flight of steps to the entrance on Regent Road. Turn left to see St Andrew's House, a magnificent art deco building built by Thomas Tait in 1939, on your right. On your left is the Old Royal High School, used as a temporary home for the Scottish Parliament before completion of the new parliament building at Holyrood. Built by Thomas Hamilton in the style of a Greek temple in 1829, it is seen by many as the city's finest neoclassical building.

Just beyond this, the road forks. Keep left on Regent Terrace and follow it around the foot of the hill as it becomes first Carlton Terrace and then Royal Terrace, an elegant Playfair-designed Georgian street overlooking Regent Gardens and London Road below.

At the roundabout at the end of Royal Terrace, turn left onto Leith Walk and head up past the Playhouse Theatre into Leith Street where you can cut up the pretty, winding road, also called Calton Hill, to return to the start point.

The First New Town

Distance 3.5km **Time** 1 hour 30
Terrain paved and mostly level

**A short, circular walk which descends by
The Mound from George IV Bridge into the
first phase of the New Town, passing some
of the city's key architectural landmarks.**

Start at the main entrance to the
Edinburgh Central Library (1887) on
George IV Bridge. Walk north across the
bridge and down The Mound, which links
the Old and New Towns. At the foot of
The Mound turn left along Princes Street,
part of James Craig's New Town, named in
honour of the sons of George III. James
Craig designed the first stage of the New
Town in 1766, winning a competition run
by Edinburgh Town Council with his plan
of two large squares and three parallel
streets between them.

To your left are Princes Street Gardens,
originally the Nor' Loch. The refuse-filled

loch was deemed a health hazard and
drained to create private gardens for
residents, allowing them to have
uninterrupted views of the castle.

At the west end of Princes Street, on the
junction with Lothian Road, is the red
sandstone Caledonian Hotel, built by the
Caledonian Railway Company to rival the
grand Victorian North British Hotel (now
The Balmoral), at the opposite end.

Designed to make the most of the castle
views, Princes Street was never especially
dignified, however. Occupants included
hair salons, coffee houses, hotels and
street traders, and the foot of The Mound
was given over to 'seedy sideshows'.

Cross Princes Street to walk up Hope
Street to Charlotte Square. Designed by
Robert Adam, it was planned as St George
Square, but renamed after the wife of
George III, Queen Charlotte, who died in
1818. On the west side is West Register

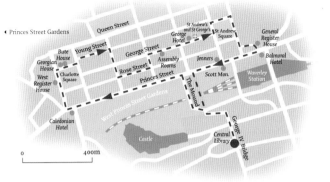

◄ Princes Street Gardens

House (1814) with its copper green dome. Formerly St George's Church, it was designed by Adam's pupil, Robert Reid and converted to a public records office in 1971. On the north side, you can get a glimpse of what life was like for residents at the Georgian House, which is owned by the National Trust for Scotland.

Leave Charlotte Square at the northeast corner to enter the narrow Young Street: like Rose Street to the south, its modest houses were designed for shopkeepers and skilled workers. Turn right up North Castle Street, left into the pedestrianised Rose Street and then left along Frederick Street, named after George III's father.

From here, turn right into George Street, the centre of James Craig's plan. Once the financial heart of the city, it is now an upmarket shopping street, its former banks converted to bars. Worth visiting are the Assembly Rooms (1787), designed by John Henderson, the former Bank of Scotland, designed by David Bryce, The George Hotel, designed by Adam and

St Andrew's and St George's Church (1784), designed by David Kay.

At the east end of George Street you reach St Andrew Square. Craig's original plan had a church on the east side, but the land was bought by Sir Laurence Dundas who built a grand mansion here. Designed by William Chambers, the house was completed in 1774, but bought by the Royal Bank of Scotland for use as their head office in 1825. St Andrew's (and St George's) Church was eventually built on the smaller site on George Street.

Leave the square at the southeast corner and turn left into West Register Street, passing General Register House, designed by Robert Adam and completed in 1786. At the east end of Princes Street is the splendid Balmoral Hotel.

Walking west along Princes Street takes you past the towering Scott Monument and Jenners, the department store and Edinburgh institution which opened in 1895. From here, it's a short walk back to The Mound.

More Grand Designs

Distance **3.5km** Time **1 hour 30**
Terrain **paved and mostly level**

A circular stroll to admire the elegant crescents and circuses of the second phase of the New Town.

After the success of James Craig's original plan for a harmonious New Town grid, based around George Street, it was decided to extend the New Town to the north beyond Queen Street Gardens. This second phase of development, during the first 20 years of the 19th century, saw the building of a series of elegant circuses and crescents. Around the same time, further construction took place to the west, creating the streets and crescents between Queensferry Street and

Haymarket. A link between the streets to the north and west of the original New Town was then created, by the building of Moray Place, Ainslie Place and Randolph Crescent, designed by James Gillespie Graham on land owned by the Earl of Moray (1531-70), the illegitimate son of James V.

Start from St Andrew Square, once one of the world's most important banking addresses. On the west side are the narrow Rose and Thistle Streets, symbolising the Union of 1707. Head west down Thistle Street, its humble tenements originally built for the New Town's lower status residents.

Turn right onto Frederick Street and left along Queen Street, named after

◀ The British Linen Bank building at 38 St Andrew Square

Queen Charlotte, wife of George III. Like Princes Street, Queen Street is built up only on one side, giving residents open views to the north across Queen Street Gardens as the land falls away to the Firth of Forth.

Continue along St Colme Street and into Ainslie Place. Turn right and leave Ainslie Place along Great Stuart Street to reach Moray Place, a grand 12-sided circus. Great Stuart Street and Moray Place are both named after the Earl of Moray. Ainslie Place is named after the Earl's second wife, Margaret Jane Ainslie.

Head clockwise around Moray Place with its circular residents' garden, and walk down Doune Terrace, which gives fine views to the north and over the beautiful private gardens that slope down

from the back of Moray Place to the Water of Leith. Continue along Gloucester Place to India Street. Turn right and walk up India Street and then left along Heriot Row. The childhood home of Robert Louis Stevenson is located at no 17.

Now take a left into Howe Street, where you can see the formidable St Stephen's Church, designed by W H Playfair, at the foot of the street, before turning right into Northumberland Street. At the end, go left down Nelson Street and then right along Drummond Place, following the curve into London Street. When you reach the roundabout, turn right up Broughton Street, with its buzzing nightlife and café culture. Turn right into Albany Street and left up Dublin Street to return to the start.

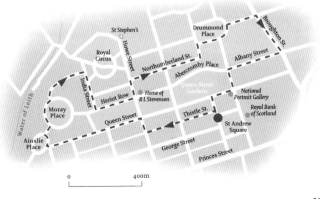

Stockbridge and the Botanics

Distance 5km Time **2 hours**
Terrain **level, can be flooded after rain**

A walk from the New Town through Stockbridge village to the Royal Botanic Garden, a must for any gardener's diary.

Start halfway down George Street at the junction with Frederick Street, where there is a statue of William Pitt, British Prime Minister 1783-1801 – one of three statues marking intersections along George Street. Walk straight down Frederick and Howe Streets towards the imposing edifice of St Stephen's Church (1827) at the foot of the hill and the smaller St Vincent's Church on your left. Now turn left into St Stephen's Street, with its bohemian mix of galleries and basement eateries, then into North West Circus Place and Kerr Street, where a small bridge takes you over the Water of Leith into the heart of Stockbridge.

Often referred to as a village, Stockbridge has a lively mix of specialist and second-hand shops, bakeries and restaurants, giving it a more laid-back feel than the grand, symmetrical streets to its south. Much of this area owes its development to the portrait painter, Sir Henry Raeburn (1756-1823), who bought two estates near here called Deanhaugh and St Bernard's, which he later sold off for the extension of the New Town.

Walk along St Bernard's Row past a small terrace of Georgian houses and,

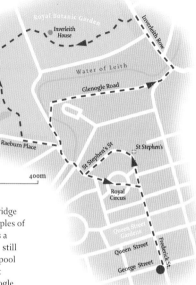

when the road splits, curve round to your right along Glenogle Road. To your left are the 11 parallel streets which make up the Stockbridge Colonies. These were laid out in 1861 by the Edinburgh Co-operative Building Company, whose aim was to create low-cost housing for working people. The cottage-style terraces of the Stockbridge Colonies are one of the finest examples of this type of housing. On the right is a Victorian red sandstone bathhouse, still in use today as a public swimming pool and home to the city's only naturist swimming club. At the end of Glenogle Road turn left into Brandon Terrace and then left again at the clock tower into Inverleith Row.

Along here on the left is the east gate of The Royal Botanic Garden and Arboretum (buses to the city centre). More than 300 years old, the Botanics have been at their present site since the 1820s. They feature several specialist gardens and are home to Inverleith House, a fine Georgian structure built in 1774. Once the Gallery of Modern Art, Inverleith House is still used for art exhibitions and has an attractive terrace café with a wonderful view south over the city. The Botanics are pleasantly laid out with ponds, a Chinese Hillside

and hothouses. The Victorian Palm House, Britain's highest, is one of the garden's most recognised features.

The main path leads you through the gardens to the west gate, where you can cross Arboretum Place into Inverleith Park. This was originally part of the Inverleith Estate, owned by the Rocheid family, and was bought by the city fathers in 1889. Cross the central tree-lined avenue to the fountain memorial, then turn left to follow the path past the pond and between the sports grounds to Raeburn Place. Turn left and follow the main road back up the hill to the New Town.

◀ The Temperate Palm House

Dean Village by the Water of Leith

Distance 5km **Time** 1 hour 30
Terrain mostly level, steps, can be muddy

**A glorious route with a countryside feel
which starts in Stockbridge to visit a city
village before returning along the Water
of Leith Walkway.**

Start in the heart of vibrant Stockbridge
on the bridge over the Water of Leith,
a 10-minute walk from the city centre
(see p30). From the west side of the
bridge, follow Dean Terrace along the
Water of Leith and up to Ann Street, one
of Edinburgh's most beautiful Georgian
terraces. Turn left into Dean Park
Crescent, then cross Queensferry Road
and take Buckingham Terrace round to
the right to reach Dean Path.

A left turn into Dean Path takes you up
to the Dean Cemetery, located on the site
of Dean House, a mansion bought by Sir

William Nisbet in 1609. Follow the main
walkway through the cemetery to a small
opening in the far wall which leads into
the grounds of the Dean Gallery. From the
steps at the front, you have sweeping
views across the lawns to the city. The
Gallery of Modern Art is on the opposite
side of Belford Road to your right: cross at
the zebra crossing to pass the sweeping
landform sculpture by Charles Jencks.

At the back, behind the café terrace,
is the car park: here, you can see the
copper-domed turrets of Donaldson's
School, built by W H Playfair. Cross the
car park to go through a gate in the wall,
then turn right along a paved path. After
passing a Henry Moore sculpture, you
then zigzag down the steps to the river
and cross a footbridge.

Turn left along the Water of Leith. (For
an alternative journey, you can turn right

◀ Dean Village

to walk upstream to Roseburn, a pretty stretch populated by rosebay and willow herb.) After the first of several weirs, cross to the left bank to continue to the stone bridge which carries Belford Road. Here, steps lead up to the Dean Gallery, where the weary can take the free National Galleries bus back to the city centre.

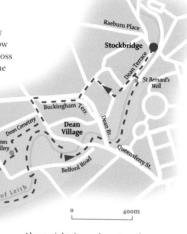

Staying on the waterside path, pass a large weir and bridge to reach a metal footbridge, where you turn steeply left to enter Dean Village. Once a successful grain-milling hamlet, it was unable to compete with Leith and eventually fell into disrepair. Today the mill buildings have been restored and converted into apartments.

Cross the bridge and turn left along a cobbled path. Over the water is the red sandstone Well Court, built 1883-86, with its distinctive clocktower. The path crosses Bells Brae where, on your left is a humble single-arched stone bridge, once the main route north out of Edinburgh.

Carry on along the Water of Leith via Miller Row to pass under Dean Bridge. Designed by Thomas Telford, this magnificent four-arched structure was built in 1832 to carry the new turnpike road over the ravine to Queensferry.

Above, right, is a 17th-century former tavern with later Baronial embellishments, whose entrance sits seven storeys up. This stretch of the Water of Leith is home to grey squirrels and foxes, as well as elm, ash and willow trees.

Further along on your left is St Bernard's Well, discovered in 1760 but reputed to date back to the 12th century. It was bought by Lord Gardenstone in 1788 who commissioned Alexander Nasmyth to design a pump room in the style of a pillared temple featuring a statue of Hygeia, the Greek goddess of health. The well was lavishly refurbished in the 19th century and in use until its closure in 1940. When you reach a stone bridge, leave the walkway by a flight of steps to return to Dean Terrace.

The Parliament and Arthur's Seat

Distance **5km** Time **2 hours**
Terrain **moderately steep, rocky paths**

**A short blast up Arthur's Seat on a
circular tour of the splendidly rugged
Holyrood Park at the heart of the city.**

This extinct volcano, rising 250m above
sea level and resembling a sleeping lion,
is one of Edinburgh's most distinctive
landmarks, and it is just minutes on foot
from the city's Old Town.

Within Holyrood Park, with the profiles
of Arthur's Seat and Salisbury Crags ever
present, is a labyrinth of paths and trails
popular with runners and walkers. Be
aware, however, that there are high crags
all around and it is not a good idea to
wander off-route or to attempt this walk

in high wind or poor visibility. Footwear
with good grip is a must.

Start from Horse Wynd in front of the
Scottish Parliament at the foot of the
Royal Mile. Designed by Spanish architect
Enric Miralles (1955-2000), the Parliament
building caused great controversy during
its construction for its unusual design and
budget-busting cost. To fully appreciate
the vision of a Parliament which 'reflects
the land it represents', however, it has to
be seen from higher ground.

To do just that, follow Queen's Drive
into Holyrood Park and turn left. Continue
past the man-made St Margaret's Loch,
created in the mid-19th century as part of
Prince Albert's improvements to the park
and home to many ducks and swans.

Where the road forks, follow Queen's Drive uphill as it curves round the edge of Holyrood Park. At the foot of Dunsapie Crag, you'll pass Dunsapie Loch and the remains of an Iron Age fort. When you reach a car park, cross the road and walk straight up the wide grass track leading to the summit.

From the top, the sweeping panorama is breathtaking: to the south the Pentland Hills, to the northeast the outer Firth of Forth and Bass Rock, to the northwest the Forth Bridges – and of course Edinburgh Castle, the Old Town and Parliament. This peak is popular at any time of day,

but sunset and early morning offer the promise of particularly enchanting views.

On leaving the summit, retrace your steps until you see the broad grass track on your left leading gently into the valley below. Follow the path as it takes you down into a second deeper valley. Continue north through this until you see a distinct earth track leading off to the right. Follow this to reach the evocative ruin of St Anthony's Chapel. Return to the valley and continue down the hill, above the medieval St Margaret's Well, one of seven holy wells in the park, to return to Queen's Drive and the start.

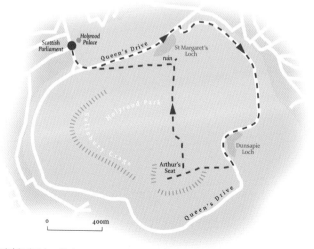

◄ Festival time in Holyrood Park

Radical Road from Duddingston

Distance **6.5km** Time **2 hours 30**
Terrain **moderate ascent and descent,
steps, grassy paths**

**An easy circular route through Holyrood
Park to Duddingston Loch, with stunning
views, birdlife and plenty of geological
and historical interest.**

Holyrood Palace sits at the foot of the
Royal Mile, just a 15-minute walk from
Waverley Station. From the palace, follow
Queen's Drive into Holyrood Park, a royal
park since the 12th century, and turn left.
Opposite the car park, take the upper of
the two surfaced paths, which leads east
and then south into the quiet valley of
Hunter's Bog, past Arthur's Seat to the
Hawse, a gap between Arthur's Seat and
Salisbury Crags. Once you're through this

gap, turn left along Queen's Drive. From
here, there are good views down to
Duddingston Village and the loch, while
above you, to the left, Iron Age cultivation
terraces are still visible.

Accompanying Queen's Drive is a low
wall and then a fence. Where the fence
ends, turn right off the road to drop
steeply downhill by a path. At the foot of
the hill, take the path which follows a
wall to the right, descending a steep flight
of steps to a car park. This is the charming
Duddingston Village. Settled since the
12th century, the village was a busy centre
for weaving in the 18th century.

Cross Old Church Lane, and head
left, to see Duddingston Kirk, a Norman
building, whose kirkyard contains 'jougs'
or stocks and a watchtower that was once
used to deter bodysnatchers, who sold
corpses to the Edinburgh medical labs.
Beyond the church is Duddingston
Manse, once home to landscape painter

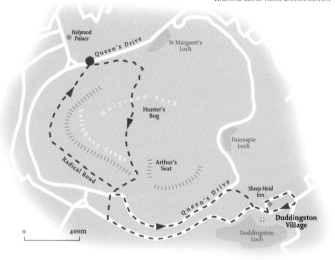

Holyrood Palace

Queen's Drive

St Margaret's Loch

Holyrood Park

Salisbury Crags

Hunter's Bog

Dunsapie Loch

Radical Road

Arthur's Seat

Queen's Drive

Sheep Heid Inn

Duddingston Village

Duddingston Loch

0   400m

Reverend John Thomson (1778-1840).

At the end of Old Church Lane, turn left up The Causeway and follow it round to one of Scotland's oldest pubs, the Sheep Heid Inn, so called because King James VI, a regular visitor, presented its landlord with a ram's head in 1580. A narrow flagstone path returns to the car park.

Now heading west, Old Church Lane passes Duddingston Loch. A bird sanctuary since 1925, and the park's only natural body of water, it is frequented by ducks and geese and provides the setting for Henry Raeburn's famous portrait of Reverend Walker skating, which can be seen in the National Gallery.

At the turn-off for the Innocent Cycle Path, formerly the route of Edinburgh's first railway line, cross the road and climb up to Queen's Drive. Instead of heading back through the Hawse, take the stony path which rises to the foot of the crags. This is the Radical Road, built at the suggestion of Sir Walter Scott. Unemployed weavers were put to work paving it after the Scottish Insurrection of 1820 in which they were involved was defeated. This route also pass Hutton's Rock, named for the scientist James Hutton (1726-97), who demonstrated the theory which forms the basis of modern geology on Salisbury Crags.

As it levels off and swings around to the northeast, the path affords magnificent views of the city below, before dropping steeply back towards the medieval St Margaret's Well, just a short way from Holyrood Palace and the start.

◄ Duddingston Loch

The distinctive line of hills, which rises abruptly to the south of Edinburgh for some 22km, serves as a unique and dramatic back garden for the capital.

These are the Pentlands, characterised by windswept moorland, grassy cleughs and glens, glinting reservoirs, acres of farmland and a network of paths and tracks. Mostly uninhabited, they represent a playground for the city's many walkers, mountain bikers and horse-riders, yet are surprisingly accessible. It is possible to get a real feeling of remoteness without ever straying too far or requiring much ascent.

But, in Edinburgh, heading for the hills isn't just about escaping the city. From its beginnings as a small settlement in the shadow of the castle, it has expanded to engulf hills like Blackford, Craiglockhart and the Braids before stopping just short of the Pentlands. These hills give a stunning vantage point from which to appreciate the capital's architectural development and its relationship with the surrounding country.

Waterways have also been integral to Edinburgh's development: the Water of Leith, which flows from the Pentlands, enables walkers to continue their wilderness journey right into town, while the Union Canal offers a great perspective on the city's industrial heritage.

Just east of the Pentland Regional Park, in Midlothian, is Roslin, an attractive village and possibly – just possibly – the final resting place of the Holy Grail.

South Edinburgh and the Pentlands

1 Union Canal and the Quay 40
Take a behind-the-scenes view of the city as you trace the route of the Union Canal over fine aqueducts to its urban heart

2 Wild Side of Craiglockhart 42
Keep your eyes peeled in this wildlife-rich nature reserve, with tree-framed views and a gentle climb over two low peaks

3 Stargazing on Blackford Hill 44
Gain a bird's eye view of the city, or indulge in a spot of stargazing, from one of Edinburgh's famous Seven Hills

4 Hermitage of Braid 46
Hide out for the day as you meander through the Hermitage Nature Reserve's peaceful wooded glen

5 A Round in the Braid Hills 48
Tee off on an easy stroll over a pair of gorse-covered hills with great views up to the Pentlands and over the Forth to Fife

6 Down in the Dells 50
Discover one of Edinburgh's best-kept secrets as you trace the course of the Water of Leith to historic Colinton

7 Currie and the Poet's Glen 52
Find inspiration on the fringes of the city with a gentle climb from Torphin, returning through a hidden glen

8 Water of Leith from Balerno 54
Join the Water of Leith for a journey through milling villages to the lovely tree-shaded Colinton Dell

9 Bonnie Bonaly and the Reservoirs 56
Gear up for a sweeping circuit of four high reservoirs through a Pentland landscape of moor, cleugh and glen

10 The Balerno Ponds 58
Admire the austere beauty of the Pentlands from a level route along Harlaw and Threipmuir Reservoirs

11 Ski Road to Swanston 60
Glide downhill from Hillend Snowsports Centre to visit Robert Louis Stevenson's idyllic country retreat

12 The Riddle of Roslin 62
Uncover the mysteries of the shady Roslin Glen with a detour to the world-famous Rosslyn Chapel and nearby castle

13 Flotterstone and the Hill Fort 64
Join this classic circuit by Castlelaw and Glencorse Reservoir, starting from an historic inn and visiting an Iron Age fort

14 North Esk Trail from Carlops 66
Venture deeper into the Pentlands from this charming Borders village to reach the shores of a birdwatching haven

Union Canal and the Quay

Distance **5km** Time **2 hours** Terrain **level**
Access **bus (44, 44A) to Lanark Road**

An urban jaunt along the historic Union Canal, starting by Kingsknowe to finish near Edinburgh's west end. This makes a great longer circuit when combined with the Water of Leith, and can be reversed to start from the heart of the city.

Built between 1818 and 1822 to transport coal to Edinburgh, the Union Canal is a contour canal, featuring aqueducts and tunnels – but no locks – along its 50km length. The waterway links Edinburgh to the Falkirk Wheel, which transfers boats from the Forth & Clyde Canal in a rotating boatlift. It is possible to cut across the entire country to Glasgow, following first the Union and then the Forth & Clyde. This route is more modest, taking walkers from one of the canal's several fine aqueducts, in the western suburbs of the city, back into town. The smooth towpath is popular with families with buggies and trikes, but is also used by cyclists and dog walkers.

Start at the footbridge that crosses Lanark Road near Kingsknowe (regular buses). Access the Union Canal towpath beneath the footbridge, and head northeast towards the city. Cross the splendid Slateford Aqueduct, 183m-long with eight arches spanning Inglis Green Road and the Water of Leith. To the right, you can see Craiglockhart Hill and

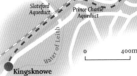

◀ Along the Union Canal

the Pentlands beyond. Next cross the Prince Charlie Aqueduct (1937) over Slateford Road, where to the left you can see Corstorphine Hill.

After passing beneath two bridges, you'll see Heriot Watt University rowing club boathouse on the left and a little further down on the right those of George Watson's and George Heriot's schools.

Lothian Road

To City Centre

Fountainbridge

Lochrin Basin

Union Canal

The canal now passes under a brightly painted bridge carrying Ashley Terrace down to Shandon.

Beyond the bridge is the Edinburgh Canal Society's boathouse with its row boats, which can be hired on Sundays, and brightly painted barges, which carry passengers from Edinburgh Quay.

To the left is the open expanse of Harrison Park. Pass under a second painted bridge with a church

above and another park to the left.

The route becomes more enclosed from here, with a wall to the left and stone-built tenements above you to the right. Passing under two further bridges, you reach the striking Leamington Lift Bridge. Built in 1896, it was moved to its current location in the 1920s and restored in 2002 as part of the Millennium Link project. Lucky visitors may get to see the bridge in operation as it lifts to allow canal boats to pass underneath. Continue past the bridge to a wide cobbled area leading up to the end of the canal at Edinburgh Quay. A recent urban regeneration programme has seen the conversion of the once industrial Lochrin Basin into offices, apartments, cafés and bars, bordering the city's financial Exchange district. From the end of the canal, bear right under the buildings and along Fountainbridge then turn left into Lothian Road, where it's a short walk to the west end of Princes Street.

To make a longer circuit, cross Princes Street at the bottom of Lothian Road and head down Queensferry Street to pick up the Water of Leith Walkway at Dean Village (see p32). Follow the Walkway westwards past the Dean and Modern Art Galleries, through Roseburn and Murrayfield and back to the Slateford Aqueduct. This circuit can also be reversed to start in the city centre.

Wild Side of Craiglockhart

Distance **4.5km** Time **2 hours**
Terrain **hilly, woodland paths, steps**
Access **bus (10, 27, 45) to Colinton Road**

A short nature walk in the wildlife-rich Craiglockhart Wood, with a climb to Easter and Wester Craiglockhart Hills for great views of the surrounding city.

One of the remarkable aspects of this nature reserve is that it is built up on all sides and yet provides an unspoilt wildlife haven and superb environment for quiet walks and recreation. The journey up the two peaks, which are often referred to in the singular as Craiglockhart Hill, give glimpses of the city from various angles.

Start by the shops in the area of Craiglockhart known as Happy Valley, on Colinton Road. Turn into Lockharton

Crescent to enter the nature reserve by the gate nearest the pond. A network of paths take you through a variety of wildflowers and trees, which include great willowherb, heath bedstraw, false oat-grass, broom, bluebell, silver birch and Scots pine. Skirt around the sheltered Craiglockhart Pond, turning right at the wall and keeping to the lower path when it splits. The pond attracts many birds including grey heron and mute swan. Kestrels also nest nearby on the hillside.

After passing a sports centre, the path climbs gently alongside Craiglockhart Wood before forking at a stone wall.

To access Wester Craiglockhart Hill, turn right and cross Glenlockhart Road to enter a wooden gate (opposite left). On your right is Napier University's

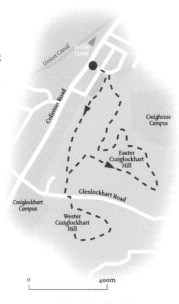

Craiglockhart Campus, the main building built as a poorhouse in 1865, later to become a hydropathic institution in 1880 and a military hospital – where the war poets Wilfred Owen and Siegfried Sassoon were sent to recuperate – in 1916. Turn left along a dirt track through trees before curving right to start your ascent. When you meet a double track, turn sharp right up a grassy path to reach the summit. Retrace your steps.

Back at the stone wall, turn right along the edge of a golf course before winding through trees. Where the path branches at a stone marker, take the right fork down a few steps and through a gap in the wall. Shortly after leaving the woods, follow a grassy track uphill (right) to a viewpoint and bench. To the south, you can see the Pentlands, to the southwest is Wester Craiglockhart Hill and Craiglockhart Campus and to the north are Corstorphine Hill and the city centre.

From here, continue eastwards by the golf course to a stone wall. Turn left through gorse to the entrance to Napier University's Craighouse Campus. These buildings were once used as an asylum and were visited by the author Joseph Conrad during his stay in Edinburgh. Turn left onto a new path between gorse and trees. When the trees end, you will see a grassy track leading to a vantage point with views to Arthur's Seat and the castle.

Return to the path and continue west. When you see the edge of Craiglockhart Wood and the gap in the wall, turn right down a grassy slope with the woodland and wall to your left. The path descends more steeply and goes down a few steps before curving right. At the foot of the hill, go through a gate in the wall and turn left to curve round to the right alongside a fence, emerging at an intersection near the pond. You can turn left here to return to the start or, to explore the small area of marsh and silver birch, turn right to return via wooden steps to Lockharton Crescent.

◄ Craiglockhart Campus

Stargazing on Blackford Hill

Distance 3km Time 1 hour
Terrain paths, moderately hilly
Access bus (41) to Cluny Gardens

A circular route round Blackford Hill and the Royal Observatory which gives splendid views of the Braid Hills to the south and the city, the Firth of Forth and Fife to the north.

Start at the entrance to Blackford Pond on Cluny Gardens, east of Morningside. Once used for curling, this is a peaceful spot for a stroll, where you can see swan, coot and moorhen. The island in the middle is a nesting site. A path runs between the pond and a wetland patch, where in spring, you can see celandine and woodland anemone, before coming to the main path that coils around the base of Blackford Hill. Follow this to the

eft to curl up around the hill to Observatory Road, where you'll see the Royal Observatory, built in 1892 when pollution from the city made the original building on Calton Hill redundant. The observatory hosts special open days and evenings, at which fledgling astronomers can take the opportunity to look at the stars through one of the country's biggest telescopes. If you detour back along Observatory Road, you can see the grand red sandstone archway at the entrance, which was built in 1887 to commemorate Sir George Harrison who enabled the city to purchase he hill as a public park.

A wide grassy path leads to the summit, where you will find a topograph and 360-degree views of the city and surrounding hills. From here, follow another broad grassy path south, then curve left round the peak on a narrow stony track, which leads to a pylon. If you wish to end the walk here, a flight of steps takes you down to the foot of the hill, where you can turn right for the pond. Otherwise, head east towards the observatory.

Skirt right around a hillock to descend south through gorse. At the end of this path, turn right along a stony track through gorse and trees. Where the path splits twice in quick succession, bear right to continue by the main path round the foot of the hill. Turn left just after the wetland patch to return to Cluny Gardens. This route can be extended to take in the Hermitage of Braid (see p46) and the Braid Hills (see p48).

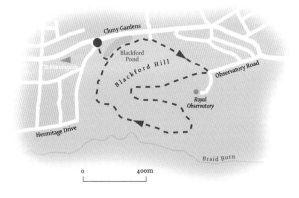

Time works for no one ...

2003

Hermitage of Braid

Distance **3km** Time **1 hour**
Terrain **level, some steps, can be muddy**
Access **bus (11, 15, 15A) to Comiston Road**

An easy stroll through a designated nature reserve, with a detour to Blackford Glen and a return journey by broadleaved woodland and wildlife-rich waterside.

This route follows the course of the Braid Burn, as it flows between the Braid Hills and Blackford Hill, making an extended hilltop jaunt an option. The name of the wooded Hermitage is thought to derive from a hermit's cell, located near here before the 17th century. Even today, you can find solitude here, but it makes for a great family nature trail with banks of snowdrops in spring, a

rich tapestry of reds and yellows in autumn, and a year-round habitat for many birds and mammals, including owl, woodpecker, vole, bat, rabbit and fox.

Start at the entrance to the Hermitage on Braid Road. A surfaced track meanders downstream along the tree-lined south bank of the Braid Burn, branching just in front of Hermitage House, completed in 1785 by architect Robert Burn for Charles Gordon of Cluny. Take the right fork to follow a stony track: you'll shortly see steps on the right leading up to an 18th-century icehouse, where ice collected in the winter was stored through summer.

Flanked by steep wooded slopes, the path now descends gently, levels off and crosses the burn by a low bridge. It

Sundial at Hermitage House

continues on the north bank, before crossing a bridge to the south and then back again by the next bridge. Shadow the north bank to Scout Bridge.

A good detour carries straight on into gorse and open ground, rising gently to Blackford Glen, and passing the old quarry and Agassiz Rock, a popular climbing spot where in 1840 Louis Agassiz found proof of the erosive action of ice. Continue as far as Howe Dean Path, which leads into the Braid Hills, then retrace your steps to Scout Bridge.

Now heading northwest away from the water, pass through a kissing gate and turn left along a wide track to go through a hole in a stone wall. The path curves to the right, rising steeply by steps before levelling off. To your right you can see

the craggy south face of Blackford Hill and to the left the Braids.

A rooty path continues through the wood, high above the glen, before starting to descend. At a fork, bear left downhill, keeping a field to your right where, at the end, you'll glimpse Hermitage House through the trees.

Take a left at the next fork to descend by a stone wall to a large doocot which contains almost 2000 nest boxes. From the front of the doocot, turn left down a flight of steps and go through a gap in a stone wall. Turn right to follow an undulating path alongside the burn and past a wildflower meadow, with one short diversion via steps, to return to the Hermitage entrance.

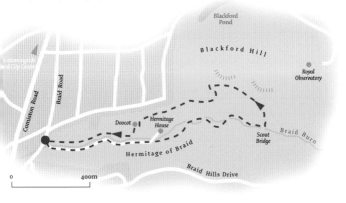

A Round in the Braid Hills

Distance 4km **Time** 1 hour 30
Terrain paths, golf course, hilltops
Access bus (11, 15, 15A) to Comiston Road

A straightforward route round the edge of the Braid Hills Golf Course, with great views of the Pentland Hills to the south and the city and Fife to the north.

Just south of Blackford Hill, across the Braid Burn, are the Braid Hills. Actually two summits, at 206m and 166m, these count as one of the Seven Hills on which Edinburgh is traditionally said to have been built, the others being Arthur's Seat, Castle Rock, Calton Hill, Corstorphine Hill, Blackford Hill and Craiglockhart Hill.

This route is easily approached from Morningside and can be combined with the Hermitage of Braid (p46) and Blackford Hill (p44) to make an exhilarating longer walk.

From Comiston Road follow Braid Hills Road and then Braid Hills Approach to the car park of the Braid Golf Club. Go through the gate and on your immediate left is a bridlepath, which takes you round the edge of the golf course close to Braid Hills Drive.

When you see Howe Dean Path leading down to the lovely Hermitage (see p46) on the opposite side of the road, turn right to cross the golf course by a broad grassy path. Where this splits, bear left for a gentle ascent, continuing south past gorse and trees until you reach a red dirt path. A right turn will take you past two radio masts, where a short detour up Buckstone Snab brings you to a topograph, the highlight of this route, with views to Blackford Hill and beyond

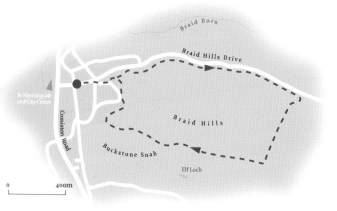

to the castle and Arthur's Seat. To the south you can see the Pentlands, to the west are the Easter and Wester Craiglockhart Hills and to the northwest is Corstorphine Hill with the Ochils in the far distance.

Rejoin the red dirt track to drop back down the gorse-covered slopes. At a fork, bear right to skirt around the back of some houses. When you meet the golf course again, turn left down a path which runs between houses and a fence to the Braid Golf Club car park. Return to the start.

◀ The Royal Observatory from the Braid Hills

Down in the Dells

Distance 3km Time **1 hour**
Terrain **moderate ascent and descent,
several flights of steps, can be muddy**
Access **bus (34, 44, 44A) to Lanark Road,
Slateford; return (10, 45) from Bridge
Road, Colinton**

**A waterside journey to Colinton Village,
passing through the quiet shade of
scenic Craiglockhart and Colinton Dells.**

The bridge that carries Lanark Road
(A70) over the Water of Leith at Slateford
marks the start of one of the most
delightful stretches of this walkway –
through the idyllic Craiglockhart and
Colinton Dells. The dells extend for more
than 2km through ancient broadleaved
woodland and along a steep gorge carved
out in the last Ice Age. Though this area is
popular with walkers and cyclists, it is
among Edinburgh's best-kept secrets, as it
is sunken, swathed in trees and entirely

hidden from the city above. Down here, it
is very hard to believe you are only ever
just a few minutes' walk from the traffic
and bustle of a busy city.

Start at the Tickled Trout pub on Lanark
Road: buses from the city centre stop
here. On the opposite side of the road,
you'll see the Water of Leith Visitor
Centre, which has an interactive exhibition
that will appeal to children, plus small
shop and café. A path skirts around the
pub beer garden towards the river, where
you'll see the first of several old mill
buildings across the water. Continue
between holly trees and, where the path
splits, follow the lower path to the right as
it descends gently towards the river.

Cross a small burn by a wooden
footbridge and continue by the main path
as it rises and then falls, keeping the
Water of Leith on your right all the while
and bearing left at a second fork. When

Water of Leith Visitor Centre ▲

Slateford

Union Canal

Water of Leith

To Balerno

Lanark Road

Redhall Mill

Colinton Parish Church

Colinton

Bridge Rd.

0   400m

To City Centre

Visitor Centre

house. At a cobbled road, bear right to follow the path up to a stony track. Turn right behind Redhall Mill House (private residence) along a narrow path, descend a flight of steps and cross a lade – a watercourse used to turn the mill wheel – via a metal footbridge. The path continues upstream between the lade and the river, before crossing the Water of Leith by Redhall Weir, where you can see the lade being siphoned off. Near here is the site of Colinton Castle, which was all but destroyed by Oliver Cromwell in 1650, only to be later part-demolished to create an atmospheric ruin for the landscape painter Alexander Nasmyth.

Turn left at the foot of a flight of steps to continue close to the water, now on the west bank as you approach Colinton. The village of Colinton grew up around its ford, an important crossing point over the Water of Leith. Its name, meaning 'village in the wood', is entirely fitting, as the old village is tucked away at the foot of the tree-shaded gorge.

Climb a steep flight of steps to meet the surfaced Dell Road, passing the historic Colinton Parish Church on the left, where Robert Louis Stevenson's grandfather, Lewis Balfour, was once minister. It's worth exploring the streets of the attractive Colinton Village, before joining the main road for buses back to the city centre.

you reach a stone bridge, bear left along the path signposted for Colinton via Kate's Mill.

After a short climb, the path splits again. Turn right to reach the waterside, where you'll see an open grassy area on the opposite bank, and continue upstream through trees on a pleasantly meandering journey. After another gentle climb, go down some steps and over a wooden bridge, before passing a white

51

Currie and the Poet's Glen

Distance **5km** Time **2 hours** Terrain **hill
paths and Water of Leith Walkway,
moderate ascent, steps, can be muddy**
Access **bus (44, 44A) to Lanark Road, Currie**

**A romantic stroll that follows the Water
of Leith from Currie, with a gentle climb
around Torphin and a return through the
idyllic Poets Glen.**

Start on Lanark Road in the suburb of
Currie, a former milling village. The
historic heart of the settlement is around
the Kirkgate, and includes the 18th-century
church, manse and cottages as well as the
Currie Brig over the Water of Leith. Go
down the Kirkgate to cross the bridge to
this conservation area.

You can access the Water of Leith
Walkway via steps or a sloping path,
which passes Currie Kirk and Manse.
Head northeast along the Walkway
towards Juniper Green. When you come to
an arched stone bridge, leave the Walkway
by a flight of steps, turning right along
the road at the top to find a dirt track
(opposite) at a sharp bend. Follow this
track, ignoring a turn-off to the right, as
you stay parallel with the Water of Leith.

Just before a house, the path swings
right, becoming stony as it rises gently.
At a second house, bear left to Woodhall
Mains, turning right onto a surfaced road
here. Just after a passing place to your
right, turn down a walled track to climb to
Torphin Quarry.

From here, go through a wooden gate,
signposted for Easter Kinleith Farm, to
follow a narrow dirt track with views

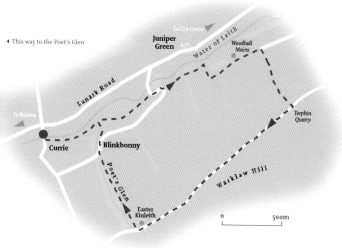

◀ This way to the Poet's Glen

Map labels:
To City Centre
Juniper Green
Water of Leith
Woodhall Mains
Lanark Road
Torphin Quarry
To Balerno
Currie
Blinkbonny
Poet's Glen
Warklaw Hill
Easter Kinleith

0   500m

across the fields to the city. After crossing a stone stile, this becomes a grassy track which rises gently to a high point, just west of the summit of Warklaw Hill. Here, you follow the right of way over a stile (waymarked) along a double track, eventually reaching Easter Kinleith Farm. Go through a metal gate and continue straight on, passing a byre on your right.

Just next to the farm steading, the road branches: bear right here and right again just before a bridge to take a narrow track, signposted 'Currie by the Poet's Glen'. This gives good views to Fife and the city as it follows Kinleith Burn, crossing one small bridge and dropping gently through trees.

Near here is the farm at Mid Kinleith, where local poet and weaver James Thomson (1763-1832), penned verses in

the Scottish vernacular about Currie and its inhabitants.

At a fork, bear left to a pool, cross a wooden footbridge and turn right to continue downstream on the opposite bank. Pass through a gap in a stone wall, keeping the wall on your right as you descend to the road. Now turn right towards the small settlement of Blinkbonny, which lies across the Water of Leith from Currie. Its cottages were built at the turn of the 20th century for workers at Kinleith Mill and Torphin Quarry.

Here, you'll find the access point for the Water of Leith Walkway (signposted) via a flight of wooden steps on your left. At the bottom of the steps, turn right along the Kinleith Burn to access the walkway, where you should turn left to return to Currie.

Water of Leith from Balerno

Distance **8km** **Time** **2 hours 30**
Terrain **level, can be muddy** **Access** **bus**
(44, 44A) to Lanark Road, Balerno

**A picturesque route along the Water of
Leith from Balerno at the foot of the
Pentlands, through several former villages
to Kingsknowe and the Union Canal.**

Balerno marks the start of the 19km
public wallkway along the Water of Leith,
although the river rises further west
above Harperrig Reservoir on the edge of
the Pentland Hills Regional Park. Balerno
began life as a farming town but, as it was
on the highest workable section of the
river, its importance grew with its mills.

This long section of the walkway is
good for families with children's cycles
and buggies, but it is also very popular
with cyclists and dog walkers.

The first stretch of this route follows
the old Caledonian Railway branch line,
which was built in 1874 to serve the mills
between here and Slateford: at one time,

the Water of Leith powered more than 100
mills. Although this upper section of the
river has long since been absorbed into
Edinburgh, there is a real sense – as you
pass through Currie, Juniper Green and
Colinton – of a series of distinct villages.

At the top of Bridge Road (near Lanark
Road) in Balerno is a signpost for the Water
of Leith Walkway. This opens out to a wide
track, which heads downstream through
light woodland, soon crossing the river to
continue on the south bank.

The track rises gently above the water,
but you can make several detours to the
water's edge, including at the Kirkgate in
Currie. Like Balerno, Currie was once a
small farming community but the village
grew with its snuff and paper mills and,
after the railway opened, became a popular
gateway for weekend visitors to the
Pentland Hills.

Soon after Currie, you pass a small weir,
where the Kinleith Burn joins the Water of
Leith from its origin in the Pentland Hills.

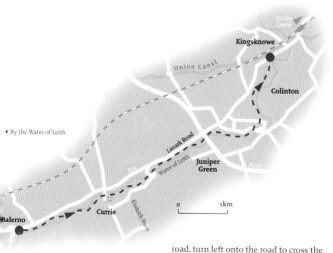

◀ By the Water of Leith

There's a turn-off here, which takes you through the peaceful Poet's Glen to Easter Kinleith Farm where you can access some of the beautiful reservoirs that nestle in the Pentlands (see p52).

Keep to the main path as the Water of Leith curves away from you, before rejoining it under the arched stone bridge carrying Blinkbonny Road. After a light woodland area, the track crosses to the north bank and Juniper Green, another attractive Edinburgh suburb and former milling village. Here, your route converges with another trail: to exit the walkway, you can take a path on the left up to Lanark Road. Otherwise, continue under the city bypass and past a weir before crossing a stone bridge to the south bank.

Where the walkway ends briefly at a road, turn left onto the road to cross the water, rejoining the walkway as it branches away to the left. You now pass Spylaw Park on the right before reaching the elegant stone bridge at Colinton Village. Ascend a flight of steps to the left if you want to exit the walkway here. Otherwise, continue through an arched tunnel to emerge high above the river on the left bank. The next stretch takes you through the glorious tree-shaded gorge of Colinton Dell. Where the path splits, bear left along the main track as it curves away from the Water of Leith.

Eventually, the walkway crosses Lanark Road over a footbridge where you can leave it and take a bus back into the city or continue on the footbridge to the Union Canal (see p40). Alternatively, you can carry on along the Water of Leith to Dean Village and Stockbridge (see p32).

Bonnie Bonaly and the Reservoirs

Distance 12km **Time 3 hours 30**
Terrain hilly, grassy paths, dirt tracks
Access bus (10) to Bonaly Road

A long circular route from the edge of
the city to explore the northern corner of
the Pentlands with its fine reservoirs and
sweeping views of the city.

Start on Bonaly Road in Bonaly: this
crosses the bypass which you then
shadow as you turn right along Torduff
Road, passing a car park and a water
treatment works as you rise gently to
Torduff Reservoir.

Go south through a gate towards Easter
Kinleith, with the reservoir on your left.
After looping around the southern end of
Torduff and crossing a bridge, the road

curves around to the right, over a second
bridge and up to Clubbiedean Reservoir,
where the waterside journey continues
with Clubbiedean on your left. At the end
of the reservoir, the road passes through
farmland, and a gate, to eventually reach
Easter Kinleith Farm and a signpost
for Harlaw.

Follow this as the road doubles back
on itself and cross the Kinleith Burn
(ignoring the sign for the Poet's Glen) to
reach a crossroads. Turn left here along a
broad stony track for Glencorse Reservoir,
4km away, past fields and a conifer
plantation on your left. After crossing a
stile, the route continues alongside a
drystane dyke, where below
to your right you can see the austere

◄ Glencorse Reservoir

Harlaw and Threipmuir Reservoirs, south of Balerno.

When you reach two metal gates, go through the one on the left to accompany a drystane dyke and a stony path over moorland and up between the low Harbour Hill and Bell's Hill. After crossing a stone stile, descend along Maiden's Cleugh towards Glencorse Reservoir. From the signpost above the reservoir, follow the grassy path as it turns back sharply on itself to the left and rises between Harbour Hill, now on your left, and Capelaw Hill on your right. Eventually, the path narrows and continues along Phantom's Cleugh. Remain on this central path as it passes the fenced conifer plantation that surrounds Bonaly Reservoir to your left. When you see a signpost for Allermuir and Glencorse, go over a stile to drop down between two plantations. Beyond the trees, you get a clear view of Bonaly Reservoir to your left. Descend by the Dean Burn and through a kissing gate, towards the city below.

After passing through another conifer plantation, a surfaced road takes you through a car park to pass the baronial mansion of Bonaly Tower, home of biographer and Solicitor General for Scotland Henry Thomas Cockburn (1779-1854). Shortly after, you reach the bridge across the bypass: cross this to return to Bonaly Road.

The Balerno Ponds

Distance **10km** Time **3 hours**
Terrain **level, can be muddy** Access **bus
(44, 44A) to Bavelaw Road**

**Starting from the gateway to the
Pentlands, this level walk loops around
Harlaw Reservoir with a detour along
Threipmuir Reservoir to Bavelaw Marsh
and the Red Moss.**

Balerno is a sprawling village on the
western edge of Edinburgh, notable for its
superb position just north of the
Pentlands. Start on Bavelaw Road, just
south of the Main Street, heading left
along Harlaw Road at a fork to continue
upstream by the Bavelaw Burn to the
Ranger Centre at the northwest corner of
Harlaw Reservoir. Harlaw and Threipmuir
Reservoirs were built in the late 19th
century to ensure a year-round water
supply for the mills on the Water of Leith.

From the Ranger Centre, follow the path
clockwise around the reservoir, through

Scots pine to the dam, built in 1848. Turn
right along the embankment to reach a
bridge and ford, and then left to skirt the
west side of Threipmuir Reservoir.

After passing through two gates (keep
closed), the path emerges onto a quiet
road. Follow this ahead and, where it
bends right, continue straight on along a
footpath through woodland to join the
road again.

On the opposite side of the road, a
raised timber walkway wends its way
across the tranquil Red Moss of Balerno, a
raised bog of heather, cottongrass and
sphagnum, which is home to dragonflies,
frogs, butterflies and many birds. A circuit
on the walkway takes 15 minutes, but it is
only wide enough for buggies as far as the
pond. This is a fragile environment, not
suitable for dogs.

Continue down the road (south) for
Bavelaw Marsh. This area, lying to the
west of Redford Bridge, is an important

■ Harlaw Reservoir

ite for breeding waterfowl with various aptors and waders also often spotted. It s best viewed from the bridge. On the other side, a driveway leads to the 16th-century Bavelaw Castle (private residence)

and there is nearby access for walkers to head deep into the Pentland Hills, where highlights include the path through the stunning Green Cleugh. If you do intend to walk into the hills from here, carry the relevant OS map and a compass.

Retrace your steps along Threipmuir Reservoir. When you reach the weir, keep left to cross the bridge to Harlaw. A woodland track leads along the western shore. At the far end, you reach another ford and narrow bridge, which you should cross to follow the path back round to the ranger centre.

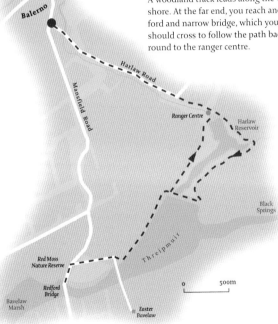

To App
and Currie

Balerno

Harlaw Road

Mansfield Road

Ranger Centre

Harlaw
Reservoir

Black
Springs

Threipmuir

Red Moss
Nature Reserve

Redford
Bridge

Bavelaw
Marsh

Easter
Bavelaw

0   500m

Ski Road to Swanston

Distance **4.5km** Time **1 hour 30** Terrain **paths and tracks, hilly** Access **bus (4, 15, 15A) to Hillend**

Skirt around the ski slope at Hillend, with wonderful views of the city and a gentle descent to the delightful hidden village of Swanston.

Start at the entrance to Hillend Country Park on Biggar Road and follow the signs for the Capital View Walk (blue waymarkers) which lead you alongside the ski centre road and then steeply left up through gorse (signposted Caerketton). Bear right towards the artificial ski slope, the longest in Britain and an Edinburgh landmark. Here, you have two choices. The easier option turns

right to skirt around the buildings at the base of the ski slope, including the headquarters of Snowsport Scotland and a café with terrace and viewing gallery over the slopes.

On the far side, a grassy track climbs to a kissing gate where a level but stony path skirts around the top of Lothianburn golf course (keep dogs on a lead during lambing). Ahead, on the small hill to your right, there's a cross-shaped copse, known as the T-wood, planted in the late 19th century to remember a fallen soldier, and the route gives stunning views across the city throughout. At a crossroads, bear right on the path signposted for Swanston and the Capital View Walk. Just to your left, the Capital View Walk is a

Cottage in Swanston's old village

reat spot for a summer's day picnic.
Alternatively, for an airy walk above the
ki centre, turn left when you reach the
ope to begin a steep ascent, bearing left
gain when you meet a path to eventually
each a stile at the top. Turn right here for
breezy stretch with stunning views
cross the city to the Braid Hills, Arthur's
eat, the Firth of Forth and beyond, with
ne golf course and wood far below as you
escend back down to the crossroads. You
an also extend the route to incorporate a
limb up Caerketton and Allermuir Hills.
From the crossroads, continue downhill
ight) by the peaceful little Swanston
urn. After passing through a kissing gate
nd crossing the burn, the path cuts
etween the golf courses of Swanston and
othianburn to reach the gate to
wanston Village.
This tiny village is an idyll, with its
rilliant white early 18th-century
hatched cottages gathered
round the burn. The cottages
vere rescued from
ereliction in the 1960s
nd are now private
omes: please respect
he privacy of
esidents on this
valk. At the north
nd, a bridge leads
ver the Swanston
urn, its banks
arpeted in pungent
vild garlic. A short

detour west will take you to Swanston
Cottage, where the village's most famous
resident once stayed. Robert Louis
Stevenson's parents leased a cottage
here in the latter part of the 19th century
in an attempt to improve their son's
health. Built in 1761, Swanston Cottage
was much extended during their stay.
There is also a converted early 18th-
century farmhouse nearby.

Back at the main collection of houses,
turn right towards Lothianburn to pass
the stone-built estate cottages of New
Swanston, which sit around a more
formal green on your right. The track
continues through the golf course to the
clubhouse, where you emerge on Biggar
Road. There's an inn here or you can
return to the café and terrace at the
Snowsports Centre just up the road.

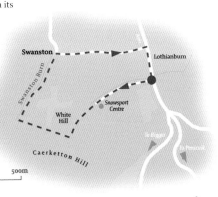

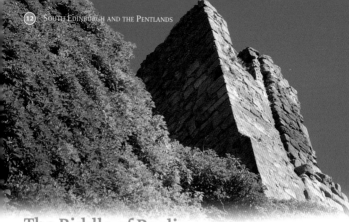

The Riddle of Roslin

Distance 7km **Time** 2 hours 30
Terrain woodland paths, can be muddy,
steps **Access** bus (15, 15A) to Roslin

**A magical journey from Roslin Village to
follow the River North Esk through the
ancient wood and nature reserve of
Roslin Glen to Rosslyn Castle and Chapel.**

Roslin may have found fame most
recently in the climax of Dan Brown's
bestselling novel *The DaVinci Code*, but the
settlement is Pictish in origin, having
reputedly been founded in 3AD, and it was
at one time the most important town in
the Lothians after Edinburgh and
Haddington. Taking its name from the
Celtic words for rocky overhang and
waterfall, this village with long-standing
literary connections nestles in the
countryside south of Edinburgh and
boasts the beautiful Roslin Glen on the
banks of the North Esk, as well as the
small but spectacular Rosslyn Chapel.

From the town centre, walk northeast
along Manse Road as it goes over a stone
bridge and through the small settlement
of Mountmarle. West of Mountmarle is
the site of the 1303 Battle of Roslin in
which 8000 Scots are reputed to have
defeated a 30,000-strong English force in
three bloody encounters during the
course of a single day.

The road becomes rougher as it passes
farm and woodland, with an outlook
towards Bilston Viaduct. Pass through a
gate to Roslin Glen County Park, where
you'll get fine views. The glen comprises
the biggest surviving tract of ancient
woodland in Midlothian, with hundreds
of species of flowering plants.

After a sharp drop, the path splits: bear
right to snake down the hill by the green
waymarker. At the foot, turn right and
pass through a wooden gate to head
upstream by the River North Esk, one of
Scotland's most romantic rivers, rising

Rosslyn Castle

bove the water on a drawn-out but
pleasant tree-lined ascent. Eventually,
he path levels off to give spectacular
views of Hawthornden Castle. This
was the home of poet William
Drummond, who built
t in 1636 around the
uins of a 15th-
entury tower.

The path now
winds through
woodland high above
he glen, before
tarting to descend back
o the water. Where it forks,
ake the higher path (right) to
se steeply past Wallace's
ave, where Scotland's
ational hero was said to
ave taken refuge during the
attle of Roslin. At the top,
he path veers away from the
iver and passes through a gap in
stone wall. Turn left into a small
learing and left at the next two forks
s you descend, then right to follow the
iver once again.

When you reach the grassy meadow by
osslyn Castle, turn right up the steps
nd pass through the stone archway to
urn right up more steps to the castle
riveway. Built after the battle of Roslin in
303, the keep of Rosslyn Castle was
argely destroyed by fire in 1544. The
ubsequent restoration included the
onstruction of a new five-storey

domestic range, the only part
that remains habitable.

At the top of the road is Rosslyn Chapel.
Founded in 1446 by Sir William St Clair,
Earl of Orkney, the building seen today is
only part of what was originally planned,
a large collegiate church devoted to
St Matthew, but is memorable for the
intricate carving inside. Venerated by both
the faithful and the mystic, it contains a
profusion of Christian and pagan
symbols, with over 100 carvings of the
Green Man and many associations with
the Holy Grail. Take the right-hand path
for a tour of this enigmatic chapel, or the
left to return to Roslin.

Flotterstone and the Hill Fort

Distance **6km** Time **2 hours**
Terrain **tarmac roads, grassy paths, moderate ascent to Castlelaw**
Access **bus (100, 101) to Flotterstone**

A classic easygoing circuit from a renowned inn to Glencorse Reservoir with a detour to the hill fort and earth house at Castlelaw.

Start at the popular Flotterstone Inn on Biggar Road (A702) between Hillend and Carlops. From the inn car park, take the road to the left of the Ranger Centre, following the blue waymarkers along the road, turning right through a gate by the signpost for Castlelaw, to climb uphill through gorse by a narrow dirt track. This emerges into open fields and ends in front of an MoD building at the top.

Turn right through a wooden gate to head east, skirting around Castlelaw Farm by a tree-lined path. Cross the road and car park to take a grassy gorse-bound path (left of the main stony track): this leads uphill to Castlelaw Hill Fort, an Iron Age fortification, and an earth house dating

from the 2nd century AD. It is thought that Castlelaw was used to store grain.

Retrace your steps and continue along the broad stony track for Glencorse reservoir (signposted), passing through a wooden kissing gate. Glencorse is one of the oldest reservoirs in the Pentland hills and is also a popular place with weekend anglers and birdwatchers.

Go through a second kissing gate and pass a conifer plantation, where another signpost for the reservoir directs you left round the trees. Turn left onto a surfaced road, which leads you along the water and past an established forest. At the far end of this, at a signpost for Flotterstone, turn right through a wooden gate, passing old filter beds. A stony track tumbles down to Glencorse Burn and carries you past a wildlife garden and two stone buildings. From this stretch, a bridge gives access to some of the highest hills in the Pentlands, including Carnethy Hill, Scald Law and West Kip (not to be explored without an OS map and compass). When you reach the road, turn right for some well-earned refreshments at Flotterstone.

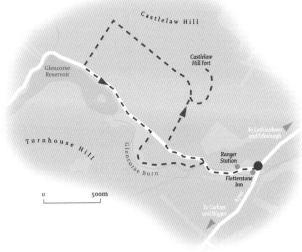

Glencorse Reservoir

North Esk Trail from Carlops

Distance **7km** Time **2 hours** Terrain **farm tracks, moorland paths, steep ascent** Access **bus (100, 101) to Carlops**

A longer circuit which heads to the bird-rich shores of North Esk Reservoir from the pretty Borders village of Carlops, returning through a quintessential Pentland landscape.

Located at the southernmost tip of the eastern Pentland Hills between Penicuik and West Linton, Carlops is an attractive village whose position on the River North Esk made it a centre for cotton-weaving: the oldest houses you see here were the original weavers' cottages. The village's most notable landmark is a rocky crag overlooking the main road, known as the Witch's Leap, from which local witches reputedly launched their broomsticks.

From Carlops Church, walk north through the village, past the old coaching inn and, beyond, along the main road (A702). At a sign for Nine Mile Burn, turn left off the A702 to shadow the road by a dirt track, before crossing a burn. When the track meets the narrow surfaced road for Patieshill Farm, bear right to keep parallel to the main road and left at the intersection with another road.

Further on, a signpost for Buteland by North Esk Reservoir via Spittal Farm leads you left along a broad dirt track. Take the right-hand path at the next junction and then right again along a public footpath (waymarked), using the left-hand path to make your ascent just after crossing a burn. After passing through a kissing gate by a cattle grid, bear left along a landrover track behind the farm, crossing the burn

▲ The village of Car

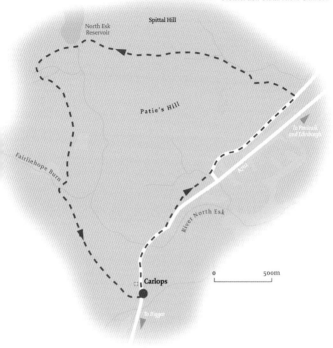

and a stile to climb between Patie's Hill and Spittal Hill, named for the hospice at its foot run by monks from Newhall in the 10th to 11th centuries.

Soon after the last cattle grid, turn left at a waymarker, following the fenceline for a while before leaving it (right). At a fork, take the lower path (left) to descend steeply to a stile and skirt around the foot of the reservoir. North Esk Reservoir, one of many reservoirs in the Pentland Hills Regional Park, is home to a large number of native and migratory birds, including the pink-footed goose, black-headed gull, mallard, tufted duck, oyster catcher, common sandpiper, redshank and cormorant.

After crossing another stile, follow a stony track signposted for Carlops, and past woods and farmland as it meanders – never far from the River North Esk – under the ridge that runs from Wether Law to Mount Maw, over a stone bridge and into the village.

East Lothian, where the land east of Edinburgh makes its gradual descent to the sea, is as much Edinburgh's weekend retreat as the Pentland Hills. Although you are never far from gentle hills, this is an altogether different landscape, with rolling arable farmland, made particularly attractive during harvest time, and a score of golf courses.

More often than not, though, it's the beaches that have residents and tourists leaving the city in droves at weekends. As well as glorious sandy beaches, East Lothian is said to have more hours of sunshine and less rainfall than any other part of Scotland.

While the land itself might lack the craggy drama of the hill country, East Lothian contains some of the most spectacular seascapes you could hope

to find anywhere, all within an hour's bus or train journey of the city centre.

The routes in this chapter pick out some of these coastal highlights for walkers: Aberlady Bay, Gullane and North Berwick all offer spectacular views, with fantastic opportunities for serious birdwatchers and detours for those who want to explore this beautiful area in more depth.

Inland and directly south of the city, in Midlothian, an 850-acre walled estate provides the setting for a family-friendly walk along the Rivers North and South Esk

Also featured in this chapter is the port of Leith. Although, unlike the other routes in this section, it is well within the city limits and accessed on foot from the centre, it remains, in many respects, apart – retaining a glimmer of proud Leith heritage and seafaring adventure.

East Edinburgh and the Coast

1 **Leith Walk to The Shore**   70
Stretch your sea legs on this tour of
Leith, once Scotland's most important
port, with a proud shipping heritage

2 **Dalkeith and the Forest of Oak**   72
Potter on the banks of the tree-lined
Rivers Esk before letting the children
loose in the timber playground

3 **Aberlady Bay Nature Reserve**   74
Tread softly to enjoy the sights and
sounds of one of the Forth's most
important sites for waders and wildfowl

4 **Gullane and the Black Rocks**   76
Breeze along this vast sandy beach and
dunes before returning to the village
green via championship golf country

5 **North Berwick Seaside Stroll**   78
Climb an iconic hill and take a jaunt
around the harbour of the town once
dubbed 'the Biarritz of the North'

Leith Walk to The Shore

Distance 6km Time **2 hours**
Terrain **paved and mostly level**
Access **regular buses on Leith Walk**

A stroll down Leith Walk and circuit of the historic port of Leith, taking in the Royal Yacht *Britannia* and The Shore.

Leith Walk, running from the east end of the city centre down to Leith, was established as a thoroughfare between fortifications on Calton Hill and the port during the Civil War. It is served by regular buses and is a short walk back up Leith Street to Princes Street and Waverley Station. Strolling down Leith Walk, you come to Shrub Place on the left hand side. In the early 18th century, market gardens developed along the length of Leith Walk and in 1764 Professor John Hope established the Botanic Gardens at Shrubhill on the west side of the road.

Leith was a separate city from 1827 until 1921 and the boundary was marked by the legendary Boundary Bar (now renamed City Limits), where when it reached closing time in Edinburgh, customers would reputedly walk to the other side of the bar and continue drinking until closing time in Leith. Further down the Walk on the right hand side is Smith's Place, bought in 1800 by wealthy merchant James Smith, who built a cul-de-sac with a large house at the end. You eventually come to Great Junction Street at the foot of Leith Walk. To detour to Trinity House, a museum dedicated to the story of Leith's maritime past, carry straight across the road and down New Kirkgate. Built in 1816, but with vaulted cellars dating from 1555 still accessible

◀ The Shore

below, it contains maritime memorabilia and portraits by Sir Henry Raeburn.

Otherwise, turn left onto Great Junction Street: here, you pass Dr Bell's School, built in 1839 to teach the Madras Education System, whereby older pupils were taught to instruct their younger peers. Continue into North Junction Street, then turn right into Commercial Street to pass the site of the former Leith Citadel, a fort built by John Mylne (1611-67).

Beyond the warehouses on the left, turn into Dock Place to reach Commercial Quay, facing the Scottish Executive building, before continuing on to Ocean Drive and the Royal Yacht *Britannia*. The *Britannia* was built on the Clyde in 1953 and sailed over 1.6 million kilometres before being decommissioned in Portsmouth in 1997.

Ocean Drive carries on to Rennie's Isle, where you cross the Victoria Swing Bridge and turn into the trendy Shore for views of the port. Leith Harbour was established around 1300 and was used for shipbuilding, whaling and commerce, particularly the importing and exporting of wine and whisky.

At the top of The Shore are a signal tower and a former seaman's mission, which is now a restaurant and hotel.

Across the Water of Leith in Commercial Street is the handsome Leith Custom House, designed by Robert Reid (1776-1856) in 1812. On the corner of Burgess and Water Street is Andrew Lamb's House, a fine example of the home of a wealthy 17th-century merchant.

Follow Bernard Street east into Constitution Street and Charlotte Street, past the grand houses overlooking the historic Leith Links, which was used first as a muster ground for troops and later as a golf course. From the south side of the links you can visit the colonies houses behind Industrial Road before returning to the foot of the Walk along Duke Street.

Dalkeith and the Forest of Oak

Distance **6km** Time **2 hours** Terrain **level, can be muddy** Access **bus (49, 86) to Dalkeith High Street**

A circular walk around the grounds of Dalkeith Country Park, an 850-acre walled estate incorporating the remnants of the Forest of Caledon.

Dalkeith Country Park evolved as a pleasure garden and working estate around the 18th-century Dalkeith House. The extensive walled parkland was enclosed in 1635 to create a deer park, and roe deer may still be spotted in the grounds. It is now managed by Buccleuch Countryside Service (entry fee may be charged to use the facilities).

From the park gates, take an immediate right past St Mary's Episcopal Church (1845) which houses a unique water-powered organ, built in Edinburgh. Follow the main road straight through the grounds of the country park, turning right onto a dirt track opposite the entrance to a timber playground.

Where this track ends, take the second path on the left to accompany the South Esk downstream, passing a small well on your left. Just up from here is the medieval Old Cow Bridge which is a Scheduled Ancient Monument. When the path is joined by another path from the left, turn right to cross the river by a footbridge and continue

◄ The conservatory

downstream, passing through a dark tunnel and climbing away from the water just before a second tunnel.

On your left a vantage point gives views across the river of the old stables (1740) by William Adam, now a bistro, and a circular stone conservatory (1832) by William Burn. Return to the path and skirt around an old amphitheatre to ascend a flight of stone steps on the far side: at an intersection turn left to cross the stone-built Laundry Bridge.

Walk past the conservatory and stables, then take a right into the trees, with open parkland on your right. You shortly intersect with an estate road that leads to the front of Dalkeith House. Built in 1701, the house incorporates the remains of the 12th-century Dalkeith Castle.

Turn right past pleasant parkland and a small picnic area. Up ahead is the Montagu Bridge (1792), designed by Robert Adam. Just before the bridge, turn right to head steeply down to the North Esk, which you now follow downstream. At a fork, bear right away from the water to zigzag up the wooded slope and along a tree-lined ridge. After dropping back down, continue straight ahead to emerge from the woods by a field. Turn left onto the main path that skirts the field: a delightful stretch through wizened oak

now follows, crossing a wooden stile and continuing above the water until you reach another stile to access a footbridge, just short of the Meeting of the Waters.

After crossing the North Esk, climb uphill (right) to an intersection, where you now turn left to return on an undulating tree-lined avenue, continuing straight across to Lugton Haugh at the first crosspath and left into the woods at the second. Bear left when you see a footbridge to follow the west side of the river downstream below Dalkeith House. When you spot the Montagu Bridge up ahead, wind uphill to meet the main estate road. Turn right to cross the bridge and right at each of the next two forks to return to the start.

Aberlady Bay Nature Reserve

Distance **6km (one way)** Time **2 hours**
Terrain **level, beach, dunes, paths**
Access **bus (124, X5) to Aberlady
and Gullane**

**A nature walk through an important
haven for birds and wildflowers and
along the coastal path to Gullane. Dogs
are not permitted on the reserve from
April to July, and must be kept on a short
lead at all other times.**

Aberlady Bay became Britain's first local
nature reserve in 1952 and is widely
regarded as one of the finest birdwatching sites in the country. The gently
shelving bay means that at low tide an
expanse of mud, grass and sand is
exposed, creating an ideal habitat for
waders. The path skirting the reserve is a
perfect spot to view birds all year round,
including curlew, greenfinch, reed
bunting, linnet, oystercatcher, redshank,
lapwing, heron, herring gull, black-headed
gull and shelduck. In summer, whimbrel,
grasshopper warblers, short-eared owl,
green sandpiper, peregrine and red-
throated divers visit the reserve.

In addition to attracting birds, the
reserve is also a haven for wild flowers,
and over 540 species have been recorded
including viper's bugloss, scentless
mayweed, ragwort, bindweed, vetch and
sea aster. The low tide also exposes the
wrecks of two WWII midget submarines.

The walk starts from the pretty village
of Aberlady: from the High Street, head up
The Wynd to the coast road (A198), which
leads northeast to a car park and long
wooden footbridge across the Peffer Burn.

Cross the bridge to take the path around
the fringes of the nature reserve, enjoying
some splendid views across the estuary to
Aberlady. The path makes a sharp right
turn, passing through sea buckthorn

◄ Aberlady Bay Nature Reserve

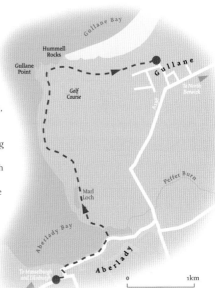

before emerging by Marl Loch, where mute swan, coot and mallard may be spotted. Follow the path along the east side of the loch, continuing north between the nature reserve and a golf course to a fork: bear left along a broad dirt track that heads west towards the sea. The path becomes increasingly sandy, passing between dunes before opening out at a wide bay. Turn right to walk up the beach or follow the path along the edge of the dunes. When you reach the rocks at the end of the beach, you'll see a path that leads you up through the dunes to the rocky headland of Gullane Point.

Bear right on a grassy path to head eastwards: at a junction, branch left down to a small beach and carry on along the coast past further small sandy coves to a rocky headland frequented by cormorants and eider ducks. Continue right around the headland to the end of the beach where a narrow path snakes uphill to a line of WWII defences. Now follow a broad sandy track heading east alongside the golf course, until you see the 12th tee, where you should turn left along a grassy coastal track. This keeps its height as it follows the coastline: at the second green

waymarker post, turn right to skirt the edge of the golf course and, at a third green post, the path bears left and becomes a broad grassy track.

Ahead you can see Gullane Bents and the dignified houses that sit on the edge of Gullane. At a junction, carry straight along the signposted path for Gullane Bents to cross a grassy slope, passing a car park and beach to the left. Turn right to reach the village and buses back to Aberlady and Edinburgh. Alternatively, you can extend your route with a loop around Gullane Bay (see p76) or continue along the coast to Yellowcraig.

Gullane and the Black Rocks

Distance **5km** Time **2 hours** Terrain **level, beach, dunes, paths** Access **bus (124, X5) to Gullane**

A short walk along the sands and dunes of the spectacular Gullane Bay, returning inland through conifers and sea buckthorn.

Gullane Bay, like neighbouring Aberlady Bay, is a wonderful place to see birds and wild flowers. In summer, the flora-rich dunes are a carpet of viper's bugloss, scentless mayweed, ragwort, woody nightshade and sea aster while birds visiting the area include curlew, oystercatcher, sandpiper, sanderling and eiders out on the rocks.

Gullane itself is a picturesque golf resort with a bustling Main Street and delightful village green. It's a short walk from here to the car park at Gullane Bents, where you follow the main path down to the beach. With its broad sweep of sand, backed by an extensive dune system and good surf, this qualifies as one of the most scenic beaches in East Lothian. Turn right and walk along the sand until the beach ends, then carry on by the path between the rocks and the foot of the dunes as it follows the coast and crosses a stony bay. Eventually, this becomes a grassy trail, which continues between a sandy cove and a conifer plantation. Pass the remains of a 16th-century chapel and accompany the grassy path down to the large sandy bay ahead.

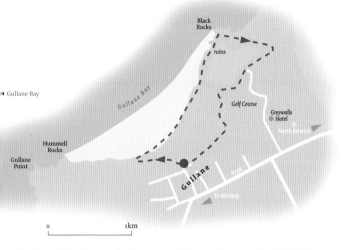

◀ Gullane Bay

At the far end of the beach, climb up into the dunes and follow the path along the edge of the beach back towards the conifer plantation. For those looking for a longer day out, it's possible to continue along the coast, passing caves and rocks, to Yellowcraig (4km), a sandy beach popular with families and dog walkers. This has a fun children's playground and great outlook to the RSPB reserve at Fidra Island, reputedly the inspiration for Robert Louis Stevenson's *Treasure Island*. From Yellowcraig, head inland to Dirleton, with its charming village green, pubs, castle and gardens, where you can return by bus.

Alternatively, to return to Gullane, turn left when you reach an area of open ground, and follow a grassy double track inland, curving round two hillocks before

splitting on the edge of Muirfield Golf Course, home to the Honourable Company of Edinburgh Golfers who wrote the first rules of the game in 1744.

Turn right and follow the path between the golf course and the conifer plantation. Just before a single-storey green building you see a signpost for Gullane Village. Turn right off the double track and follow this path into the conifer plantation, bearing left before emerging from the trees and continuing on a sandy path flanked by sea buckthorn. This skirts the golf course before widening into a bridlepath and curving inland. When it splits, bear left on the bridlepath as it rises up past a grassy tree-lined area before arriving at the edge of Gullane Village. Return to the centre of the village for buses back to Edinburgh.

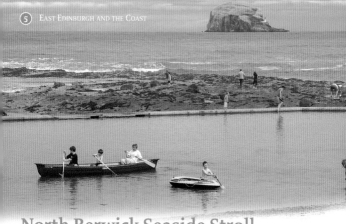

North Berwick Seaside Stroll

Distance **7km** Time **2 hours**
Terrain **roads, grassy tracks, steep ascent**
Access **regular trains to North Berwick**

An exhilarating walk around some of the highlights of North Berwick, including its harbour, beaches, golf links and award-winning seabird centre, with a detour to the top of an iconic hill.

From the train station, walk southeastwards along Station Road, Marmion Road and Clifford Road before turning right to head south along Law Road. At a sharp right bend, take the rough road signposted for North Berwick Law. When you reach a car park, cross to the far side where a gap in the wall gives access to a stony track. Turn right along this and when it forks, take a left to follow a widening path. At the next two junctions turn left to wind your way up to the summit (don't wander too far, as there are steep crags to the south).

One of the impressive features of North Berwick Law is the arch made from a pair of whale jawbones, which can be seen from miles around. There have been whale jawbones here for almost 300 years, the first placed in 1709 and the current ones in 1935. Equally spectacular are the views. To the north is North Berwick, the Bass Rock and Fidra Island, to the east Tantallon Castle, to the south Traprain Law and to the west Arthur's Seat, where Edinburgh Castle can also often be seen.

Retrace your steps to the intersection with Clifford Road and turn right along St Baldred's Road. Turn left into the grounds of North Berwick Lodge (signposted). Choose the right-hand path to head seaward through the centre of the park, passing a crazy golf course and a natural arch formed by two trees. A left turn will take you around the back of the white 18th-century townhouse of the Hamilton Dalrymple family and through a

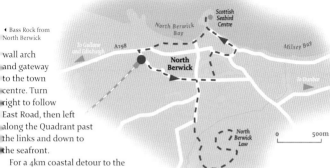

◄ Bass Rock from
North Berwick

wall arch
and gateway
to the town
centre. Turn
right to follow
East Road, then left
along the Quadrant past
the links and down to
the seafront.

For a 4km coastal detour to the
dramatic red sandstone ruin of Tantallon
Castle, turn right. Otherwise turn left
along Melbourne Road for a short blast of
sea air, bearing right, out on to the
promontory, to pass the site of St
Andrew's Old Kirk. The church was built
in the 12th century, but collapsed into the
sea in the 17th century. All that remains is
the porch and ruined walls.

No trip to North Berwick is really
complete without a visit to the Scottish
Seabird Centre, out on the promontory.
The beautifully designed building houses
a wildlife-viewing centre with close-ups,
via live webcams, of the hundreds of
thousands of seabirds that make the Bass
Rock, Fidra Island and the Isle of May
their home at various times of year. Some
5km offshore from North Berwick, the
Bass Rock is a volcanic plug with sheer
cliffs rising straight out of the water to
100m. It is the largest single rock gannet
colony in the world, as well as being
home to guillemots, razorbills, herring
gulls, puffins, shags, kittiwakes and terns.
Such is the density of its seabird

population that from the coast it appears
snow-capped. Cameras are also trained on
the Isle of May, further out in the Forth,
where early in the year, you'll see
thousands of puffin spring-cleaning their
burrows and, in late autumn, grey seals
and their pups. The Centre has a shop and
cafe with a deck overlooking the sea.

After leaving, cross the green and go
between two buildings to the harbour,
where a path leads to a rocky outcrop for
more views of the Bass Rock: boat trips
also operate from near here in summer.

Return to the harbour entrance and
walk west along the sand or along Forth
Street and then through the links. to the
end of the path at Beach Road. Turn right
past the North Berwick Golf Clubhouse.
This opened in 1880 on the site of the Old
Toll House where travellers entering the
town paid a road tax. In 1969 the tolls
were abolished and the building was
demolished. Walk straight up Station Hill,
turning left to reach the station.

The Firth of Forth, stretching for almost 90km from Stirling to Dunbar, has been an important shipping area since Roman times and a constant presence in the history and fortunes of the city for which it forms the natural northern boundary.

To the northwest of the city, between the picturesque villages of Cramond and South Queensferry, you will find some of the most scenic stretches of the inner firth, where it is possible to appreciate its function as a wildlife haven as well as a communications and shipping route.

Of course, there is evidence of the latter too and you are likely to see tankers – as well as yachts and perhaps the ferry from Belgium – on the walks in this chapter.

Another notable river, the Almond,

forms the basis for four of these routes, including a journey around Cammo Estate and a trip to Cramond itself, figuring briefly in a longer excursion from the Forth Rail Bridge and, further up in West Lothian, the hidden gem that is Almondell & Calderwood Country Park.

Also out west, you can combine a classic circuit of the royal park and palace of Linlithgow with a stroll along the Union Canal, while, in the Bathgate Hills above, Beecraigs Country Park is the setting for some family fun.

Much closer to town is Corstorphine Hill, one of the Seven Hills on which the capital is founded and within roaring distance of the city's favourite children's attraction – Edinburgh Zoo.

Cramond Island from Silverkn

North and West Edinburgh and beyond

1 **Corstorphine Hill Safari**   82
Go wild in a wooded hilltop maze for
splendid city viewpoints and sightings
of Edinburgh's zoo inhabitants

2 **Cammo Curiosities and
the Almond**   84
Seek out traces of a glorious past around
the ruins of what could well have been
the inspiration for the House of Shaws

3 **Silverknowes to Cramond Island**   86
Scour the shore from Silverknowes to an
ancient settlement and, if the tide is with
you, make an exciting detour out to sea

4 **South Queensferry
to Cramond Brig**   88
View an iconic bridge from below,
passing castle and grand estate as you
explore this bird-rich coast to Cramond

5 **Linlithgow Palace and
the Union Canal**   90
Admire the magnificent ruins of the
birthplace of Mary Queen of Scots after
cruising along the Union canal

6 **Beecraigs Loch and Cockleroy**   92
Spot deer and ducks as you stalk round
this loch in a country park, with an
optional climb of Linlithgow's own hill

7 **Bridges of Almondell**   94
Leave the city for a family walk and
picnic in a less-known country park on
the peaceful banks of the River Almond

Corstorphine Hill Safari

Distance **3km** Time **1 hour** Terrain **hilly, grassy paths, steps** Access **bus (41) to Queensferry Road**

A short route that winds along the top of Corstorphine Hill via the Scott Tower, with optional detours to the south end of the ridge and Edinburgh Zoo.

Corstorphine Hill, which stands just 161m high, rises above the northwestern suburbs of Edinburgh as a long L-shaped ridge, with a dense cover of trees. It has been designated a nature reserve because of the colonies of badgers living on the slopes of the hill and is also home to a wide variety of native trees and flowers.

Start just west of the Quality Street junction on Queensferry Road, where a wide signposted path leads from the south side of the road. When it splits, bear left to skirt around the hill and at the next intersection, turn right and continue past a field to climb a steep slope and flight of wooden steps. At the top, turn left for a further climb before the path levels off, rewarding you with views east across Murrayfield Golf Course to the city centre, Arthur's Seat, the castle and the Firth of Forth. The path now swings round to the right and forks. Bear left to follow the path high above the golf course with views north to Granton, Cramond and Fife. Still skirting the golf course, the path swings right and rises over stony ground.

Immediately south of here is Edinburgh Zoo, founded in 1909 and home to over

,000 animals.
A popular
attraction is the
penguins, which gather
together for a daily parade
outside their enclosure. You
an detour to the perimeter for
chance sighting of some of the
nhabitants: this part of the
idge is known as Rest-and-be-
hankful as it was where
ravellers paused for their first
iew of the city.

To visit the zoo itself, leave the
ill by Kaimes Road to turn left
long Corstorphine Road: this
makes a wonderful, family-friendly
detour, but allow at least half a day
regular buses back to the city).

Alternatively, turn right at the top
o follow a fence west and up and
lown some steps. At a crosspath,
urn right uphill to pass a striking
tone tower and a pylon to your left.
he Corstorphine Hill Tower, also
nown as the Scott Tower or
lermiston Tower, was built as a
memorial to Sir Walter Scott in the 1870s.

A steep descent is followed by an
ndulating stretch, with some gentle
limbs to reach the high point, where the
ath winds through gorse. An open grassy
illock gives sweeping views across the
ty to Arthur's Seat. Bear left to maintain
eight as the path wanders through trees
nd then gorse. Start to descend, with
views west to Cammo Estate, the airport
and the Pentland Hills. When the path
splits, bear right down a wide track,
keeping a disused quarry on your left,
to return to the road.

Edinburgh Castle from Corstorphine Hill

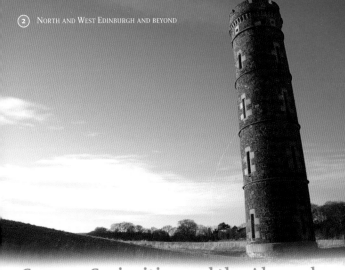

Cammo Curiosities and the Almond

Distance **8km** Time **2 hours 30**
Terrain **steep incline near the start, then level, can be muddy** Access **bus (43) to Cramond Bridge**

A long walk to explore the hidden delights of Cammo Estate and the peaceful banks of the River Almond: this can also make two shorter routes.

Start at the Cramond Brig hotel on Queensferry Road where a minor road skirts behind the hotel to Old Cramond Brig. This was built in the 16th century and comprises three arches with massive triangular cutwaters. King James V was reputedly attacked whilst crossing it and had to be rescued by a local farmer.

Cross the bridge and go right to access the River Almond Walkway. This takes you under the new Cramond Bridge and the busy Queensferry Road and continues upstream to Cammo Road. Turn left along the road to reach the entrance to Cammo Estate. The estate has been gifted to the public as a wilderness park and is popular with birdwatchers as well as local dog walkers. A straight tree-lined route, the remains of the original lime avenue, leads past fields where, on the left, you'll see an old castellated water tower, one of several architectural curiosities on the estate.

The ruins of Cammo House are at the head of the avenue. Built for John Menzies in 1693, the house was inhabited until 1975 when it was bequeathed to the National Trust for Scotland. Unfortunately, a fire left it derelict soon after and it has since been almost

◄ Cammo Tower

completely demolished with only the lower section of the walls of the house surviving, raised on a grassy knoll.

Once one of Edinburgh's most elegant houses, its chequered history and gradual decline have led to claims that it was the model for the House of Shaws in Robert Louis Stevenson's classic tale *Kidnapped*.

The parkland surrounding the house was laid out between 1710 and 1726 by amateur architect Sir John Clerk of Penicuik (1676-1755) and contains some fine specimen trees, including a very large ash which is thought to be the oldest in Edinburgh.

From the ruins, turn right and follow a dirt track through a kissing gate to skirt around the edge of a field, bearing right at the top to exit and cross Cammo Road.

You'll find a track on the other side, which takes you to the old stone Grotto Bridge over the River Almond. You can either cross here to follow the path back to the Cramond Brig, or head upstream along the Almond gorge to eventually reach a railway bridge.

Turning left to follow the railway, you will soon be under the flight path of Edinburgh Airport. Continue (left) to Lennie Mains where you should take the first left to Nether Lennie. A right turn will take you back to the River Almond Walkway. When you reach the Grotto Bridge, cross the water and turn right to return to Cramond Bridge.

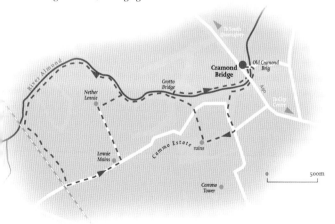

Silverknowes to Cramond Island

Distance **7km** Time **2 hours 30**
Terrain **level, can be muddy in winter,
check tide times before heading out to
Cramond Island, leave time for return!**
Access **bus (42) to Marine Drive; (43)
return from Cramond Bridge**

**A shoreline walk from Silverknowes to
the historic port of Cramond and along
the River Almond to Cramond Bridge,
with optional detours to Lauriston Castle
and Cramond Island.**

Start at the roundabout on Marine Drive
in Silverknowes, where a footpath leads
down to the seafront and joins the coastal
path to Cramond. If you have time, it is
worth making the 1km detour from the
start to the Edwardian country house of
Lauriston Castle, which boasts a fine
collection of tapestries, paintings and
porcelain (head south along Silverknowes
Road from the roundabout and take the
footpath on the right).

Back at the shore, follow the coastal
path westwards: on a clear day the views
across to Fife are terrific. The path ends in
the historic port of Cramond where, if the
tide is out, you can enjoy an exciting walk
along the causeway to Cramond Island,
inhabited until 1947 and a favourite haunt
of Robert Louis Stevenson when he was a
boy. It is vital to check tide times before
attempting this as the causeway is
submerged during high tide. The island
was fortified at the outbreak of World War
II and the gun emplacements and
buildings that housed stores and shelters
can still be explored by visitors.

◀ Cramond Inn

Arriving at the village, turn up Cramond Glebe Road. On your left is the lovely Cramond Inn, dating from the mid-17th century with later additions: it was frequented by Robert Louis Stevenson as a young man. Further up the road is a car park, where you can see the remains of a Roman bathhouse, and beyond this on the left hand side is the attractive Cramond Kirk, built in 1811.

The road immediately before the church on the left leads to the H-shaped Cramond House, built in 1680. Beside the house are the remains of a Roman fort, dating 2 AD. Recent excavations around the fort revealed evidence of human activity in the area dating back to 8500 BC, making this the oldest site of human habitation found in Scotland. Retrace your footsteps back down to Cramond Village and turn left. At the mouth of the River Almond is Cramond Boat Club, home to the few remaining boats in this once busy harbour.

A riverside path leads upstream past the boat club, passing the ruins of Caddells Forge – a water-driven ironworks – and Caddells Row, where the ironworkers lived. Before the 1820s, there were five mills on this stretch of the Almond, producing items such as nails, barrel hoops and anchors.

When you reach Old Cramond Brig, which has been in use since 1500, turn right across the bridge and follow the road up to the Cramond Brig Hotel, where you can catch the bus back to the centre of Edinburgh.

South Queensferry to Cramond Brig

Distance 11km **Time** 3 hours **Terrain** level, but can be muddy **Access** train to Dalmeny; bus (43) from Cramond Bridge

A long walk that starts in an historic harbour town before exploring the shoreline past Barnbougle Castle and Dalmeny House to the mouth of the River Almond and Cramond Bridge.

South Queensferry is defined by its position beneath the awe-inspiring rail and road bridges on the Firth of Forth, but this town is worth exploring for its combination of history and seaside atmosphere alone. From Dalmeny train station, walk along Station Road and turn right into The Loan to join the High Street. Across the road, Harbour Lane leads down to the water. In the 19th century, Queensferry was famous for its young herring, known as garvies, and for whisky.

Further east along the High Street, you will see Black Castle where, in the 18th century, barrels of contraband brandy were rolled along an underground passage to the harbour. Continue past

a series of interesting buildings and along the seafront to Hawes Inn. Dating back to the 17th century, it was a favourite haunt of Robert Louis Stevenson and is believed to have provided some of the inspiration for his book *Kidnapped*.

Here, you pass under the Forth Rail Bridge, one of the world's great feats of modern engineering, completed in 1890. Continue east along the shore to Long Craig Pier, where a gate gives access to the grounds of Dalmeny House. Take the coastal path through woodland to Hound Point, reputedly haunted by the dog of Sir Richard Mowbray, a knight killed in the Crusades. The Point affords spectacular views across the water to Fife and down to Barnbougle Castle, while the narrowing of the firth makes it a great place to

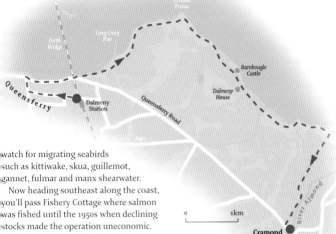

watch for migrating seabirds such as kittiwake, skua, guillemot, gannet, fulmar and manx shearwater.

Now heading southeast along the coast, you'll pass Fishery Cottage where salmon was fished until the 1950s when declining stocks made the operation uneconomic. Stroll through woodland to meet a surfaced road, signposted Shore Walk, and continue to Barnbougle Castle. This was the original home of the Earls of Rosebery. Built by the Mowbray family on the site of a medieval towerhouse, the castle, was destroyed and rebuilt in the 19th century, but then abandoned for the more comfortable surroundings of Dalmeny in 1817. In 1881, the fifth Earl of Rosebery rebuilt the castle as a retreat and to house his library. Today, Barnbougle is the main Rosebery family residence.

Beyond Barnbougle, you can view the impressive Tudor gothic Dalmeny House across its sweeping lawns. Turn left here to follow a grassy track north to the sea, passing a sandy beach before accompanying a burn upstream to a small footbridge. A grassy track heads eastwards through the trees. When you reach some houses on your left, cross a surfaced road and continue along the track, signposted Shore Walk Cramond Ferry, as it leads pleasantly through woodland before rising gently to Snab Point. The coastal path soon passes a beach frequented by curlew, sandpiper and oystercatcher, and then Eagle Rock, whose name comes from the eagle carved on it, possibly by Roman legionaries.

Where the path splits, take the right fork to leave the coast and meet a gravel road, continuing southwest between fields and past houses to East Craigie Gate. Turn left to follow the River Almond Walkway to the historic Cramond Brig Hotel and buses back to Edinburgh.

◀ The Forth Rail Bridge

Linlithgow Palace and the Union Canal

Distance **6km** Time **2 hours**
Terrain **mostly level, avoidable steps**
Access **regular trains to Linlithgow**

A great circuit that combines a classic loop of Linlithgow Palace and loch with a short stroll along the Union Canal and a glimpse of the town's historic High Street.

From the westbound platform of Linlithgow railway station, turn right up Back Station Road to reach the canal basin and its brightly painted barges. Boat trips from the Canal Centre run at weekends in summer, and there's a seasonal tearoom and museum. Opposite the basin is an unusual 16th-century beehive doocot with 370 nesting boxes.

Walk west along the towpath until you are almost at a stone bridge, where you leave the canal and turn right down Friars Brae and then left along Royal Terrace, which runs parallel to the railway. Cross

the railway by a footbridge and head down Lion Well Wynd to reach the High Street.

On turning right into the High Street, you will see St Peter's Episcopal church Church on the right. On the same side is the 18th-century Georgian Annet House. Now a local history museum, it features a statue of Mary Queen of Scots in its pretty rear garden. Next comes the Sheriff Court, with a plaque marking the site where the Earl of Moray was assassinated in 1570.

Take care when crossing the road to the Cross Well, also known as Linlithgow Cross, which stands at the centre of an impressive square. Built in 1807 by Robert Gray, a one-handed stonemason, as a replica of an earlier well built in 1628 on the same spot, it includes carvings of St Michael, a piper and drummer and is crowned by a unicorn signifying Linlithgow's royal past.

Enter the square, turn left before the Kirkgate to cross a car park where, at

▲ Linlithgow Loch

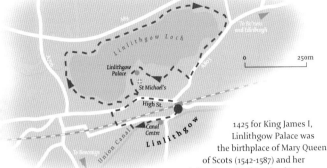

the far side, some steps lead down to Linlithgow Loch. (To avoid these steps, return down the High Street, where there are several access points to the loch.) Turn left and follow the waterside path past a small playground and area populated by swan, mallard duck and greylag geese.

The path continues to run close to the edge of the loch on the wilder, reed-fringed north side, affording spectacular views of Linlithgow Palace. The two larger islands you'll see from here are crannogs, ancient defensive loch dwellings built some 2000 years ago.

Eventually, the path meets a road. Either turn right to reach the main road and then follow this to the right again, or cut through Fiddler's Croft, a lochside meadow, which meets the main road further down (keep dogs on a lead).

From the main road, turn right down a walled path just before St Michael's Catholic Church to enter Linlithgow Peel, one of only two royal parks in Scotland: turn left to reach the palace. Built from

1425 for King James I, Linlithgow Palace was the birthplace of Mary Queen of Scots (1542-1587) and her father James V of Scotland (1513-1542), and was visited by Bonnie Prince Charlie in 1745 before burning down a year later. Much of the original structure remains, including the chapel, courtyard and roofless great hall. In front of the palace is St Michael's Parish Church. Dating from 1425, the church has been a meeting place for the General Assembly of the Church of Scotland and a haven from the plague. The spectacular metal spire was added in 1964 and, inside, there is a stained glass window designed by noted Pre-Raphaelite artist Edward Burne-Jones (1833-1898).

Returning to the Kirkgate in front of the palace, you will see the Burgh Halls, built in 1668 on your left and Cross House, dating from around 1700, on your right. From here, turn left along the High Street, passing 16th-century Hamilton's Land and, further down, St Michael's Well, dating from 1720. To return to the start, cross the road at the corner pub, just before the roundabout, where a small side street leads back up to the station.

Beecraigs Loch and Cockleroy

Distance 5km from Park Centre
(+3km Cockleroy detour)
Time 1 hour 30 from Park Centre
(+1 hour 30 for Cockleroy detour)
Terrain mostly level paths and tracks,
steps, moderately steep climb on detour
Access footpath from Linlithgow

A family-friendly forest and lochside
walk through Beecraigs Country Park,
passing a deer farm and fishery, with an
optional hilltop detour.

Beecraigs Country Park covers some 913
acres of predominantly managed
woodland in the Bathgate Hills, its
labyrinth of trails taking you deep into
shaded pine forest. To approach on foot
from Linlithgow train station (4km), head
up to the canal basin (see p90) and then
west along the towpath to Preston Road.
Turn left here for a stretch of pavement
and then roadside walkway; shortly after
this ends, a rougher footpath dives into
Hillhouse Wood on the left. You emerge at
a road junction at the top to follow the
road straight across (signposted Beecraigs
Loch), passing a restaurant (right) before
reaching the Park Centre on the left.

From this small wooden lodge, head
for the deer viewing bridge in the far
right corner of the car park, where a track
leads down past the deer farm to
Beecraigs Loch (keep dogs on a lead
here). The autumn rut is a particularly
good time to visit, when you might be
lucky enough to witness some loud
bellowing, posturing and open hostility
among the stags as they attempt to

◄ Beecraigs Loch

defend their hinds against competition.

Head clockwise (left) around the loch, through woodland to emerge at the dam. All-terrain buggies can negotiate the lochside loop, though you will have to descend some steep steps here. Stocked daily with rainbow trout, this is a popular spot for fly fishing and there is a small educational centre (left) where you can feed the fish. After crossing the dam, the route continues easily along the southern shore, with good information panels for budding duck-spotters.

When you reach the road, cross to the car park entrance opposite, where (to avoid a short stretch of road walking) a path loops left across a wooden bridge and up a few steps, emerging on the signposted track to Balvormie. This wide tunnel-like track, with its carpet of pine needles, leads you through conifers to Balvormie car park and Mill Pond, a sunny picnic spot, just across the road.

For a detour with stunning views, head past the pond to the furthest right of several tracks (light blue waymarkers) which, after passing the toilet block, ducks back into the dark, atmospheric forest: keeping to the main track, you pass through a kissing gate, cross a road and continue to a stile where, beyond, a broad grassy path takes you to the top of Cockleroy. The ridge at the summit gives spectacular views over the surrounding countryside. On a clear day you can see the Isle of Arran, Ben Lomond, Arthur's Seat, Bass Rock and the Forth Bridges.

Retrace your steps to Balvormie car park where, in the northeast corner, there's a fine adventure playground. Directly alongside this, a broad forest trail leads back to the Park Centre.

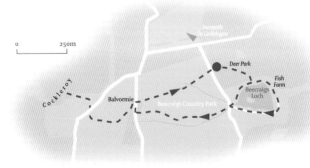

Bridges of Almondell

Distance 4km **Time** 1 hour 30
Terrain woodland paths, can be muddy,
steep section to start, avoidable steps
Access bus (27, 28, X25) to Mid Calder

A riverside walk through the picturesque Almondell & Calderwood Country Park, with glimpses of West Lothian's engineering history and rich wildlife.

Though it extends for more than 4km along the course of the River Almond and its tributaries, Almondell & Calderwood Country Park remains one of the little-known gems of West Lothian. This route explores the 97-acre Almondell estate, whose visitor centre, picnic areas, barbecue sites and buggy/trike-friendly trails make it a perfect family destination.

The route starts in Mid Calder (shops, pubs). From the bus stop in the village

centre, head east past the Torphichen Arms and over the bridge: on the far side you'll see a path on the left. Cross the busy B7015 here to follow the Calder Water a short way before climbing a few steps to the main path to Almondell. (To avoid the steps, head up the B8046, signed Pumpherston, just before the bridge, where you'll see a car park and the start of the main path on the right.)

From the steps, turn right to follow an asphalt path on a steep, steady climb (wooden handrail) before dropping back down and passing two weirs. At the second weir, cross the River Almond, and continue downstream beneath a high viaduct. This was built in 1885 to service various quarries, brickworks, mines and oil works in the area and, though it closed in 1956, it is still open to pedestrians.

◀ Nasmyth Bridge

Soon, you come to an aqueduct. Built during the construction of the Union Canal, it carries the canal feeder stream over the River Almond in a cast iron trough. After crossing here, bear left to accompany the feeder stream across a large, open picnic area as you approach Almondell Bridge, better known as Nasmyth Bridge, as it was designed by the influential Scottish landscape painter and architect Alexander Nasmyth.

Rather than crossing this bridge, continue over a road and along a narrow, uneven path on the east bank. (An easier option for the less footsure, is the red ash path further up the hill, but families with buggies or trikes should cross the bridge to continue.) After crossing a burn, this rooty path winds up through trees to the top of the ridge, which it now follows left to run high above the water.

Descend by a flight of steps to the River Almond, turn left and cross the water by the Mandela suspension bridge. Continue straight on past the former walled garden, now a lovely picnic and play area, turning left to reach the former coach house, now a visitor centre with small aquarium, exhibition and basic refreshments.

To return, the waymarked red route heads easily through rhododendron bushes, crossing a burn and passing rapids. When you reach Nasmyth Bridge, leave the surfaced path to take a waterside path signposted Mid Calder. Keep to this bank until you reach your original crossing at the weir, then return over the water to the start.

For an alternative walk, the adjoining 130-acre Calderwood is also accessed from Mid Calder. A natural plateau between the Linhouse and Murieston Waters, it has been left undisturbed to create a wildlife haven and you'll find a network of rough paths diving off into this mix of wizened birch, oak, hawthorn and scrub.

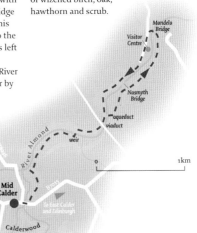

Index

Aberlady	74
Almondell & Calderwood	
Country Park	94
Arthur's Seat	34, 36
Balerno	54, 58
Bavelaw Marsh	58
Beecraigs Country Park	92
Blackford Hill	44, 46
Blackford Glen	46
Blinkbonny	52
Braid Hills	48
Broughton	20, 28
Bruntsfield	22
Bonaly	56
Caerketton Hill	60
Calderwood	94
Calton Hill	24
Cammo Estate	84
Carlops	66
Castle Rock	10, 12, 14
Castlelaw Hill	64
Clubbiedean Reservoir	56
Cockleroy Hill	92
Colinton	50, 54
Corstorphine Hill	82
Craiglockhart	40, 42
Cramond	86
Cramond Bridge	84, 86, 88
Currie	52, 54
Dalkeith	72
Dalmeny Estate	88
Dean Village	20, 32
Duddingston	36
Flotterstone	64
Fountainbridge	40
George Street	26, 30
Glencorse Reservoir	56, 64
Grassmarket	10, 18, 22
Gullane	74, 76
Harlaw Reservoir	58
Hermitage of Braid	46
Hillend	60
Holyrood Park	34, 36
Juniper Green	52, 54
Kingsknowe	40, 54
Leith	70
Linlithgow	90, 92
Lothianburn	60
Marchmont	22
Meadows, the	22
Mid Calder	94
Morningside	22
Mound, the	14, 18, 20, 26
North Berwick	78
North Esk Reservoir	66
Princes Street	14, 16, 26
Red Moss	58
River Almond	84, 86, 88, 94
Roslin	62
Royal Botanic Garden	30
Royal Mile, the	10, 12, 14, 16, 18
Silverknowes	86
Slateford	40, 50
South Queensferry	88
St Andrew Square	26, 28
Stockbridge	20, 30, 32
Swanston	60
Threipmuir Reservoir	58
Torduff Reservoir	56
Torphin	52
Union Canal	40, 90
Warklaw Hill	52
Water of Leith	20, 32, 50, 52, 54
Yellowcraig	76